THE UNITARIAN WAY

The Unitarian Way

Phillip Hewett

Blackstone Editions

Blackstone Editions
Providence, Rhode Island & Toronto, Ontario, Canada
www.BlackstoneEditions.com

© 1985, 2015 by Phillip Hewett. All rights reserved

The first edition of *The Unitarian Way* was published by the Canadian Unitarian Council in 1985. The second edition was published by Blackstone Editions in 2015.

Printed in the United States of America

ISBN 978-0-9816402-2-8

Contents

Preface	vii
1. An Epoch of Homelessness	1
2. Where Can We Look For Guidance?	12
3. The Charter of Freedom	24
4. The Reunion of the Separated	32
5. Circles, Poles and Spheres	41
6. The Unitarian Dance	52
7. Maps, Metaphors and Myths	61
8. Inter-Religious Dialogue	73
9. The Spirit of the Age	84
10. What Do Unitarians Believe?	100
11. Wider Horizons	112
12. Dimensions of Community	123

Preface

The purpose of a preface, as I understand it, is chiefly to give prospective readers some indication of what they will be likely to encounter if they should decide to invest time and attention in going further into the text. The subject-matter of this particular book is broad – as broad as life itself. It describes an approach to life, to the problems and dilemmas it presents and to the attempt to live it meaningfully and deeply, that will be found among people who call themselves Unitarians.

Such people vary widely in their individual convictions and lifestyle, but there are certain common elements that make the use of the one name appropriate. The extent to which it is appropriate may vary from one person to another. There is no sharp distinction between "sheep" and "goats." Some people take a long time to decide whether or not they are in fact Unitarian. You may feel that you are in that situation, or you may be reading in a more detached way. In either case, what follows is intended as one half of a dialogue to which you provide the other half as you proceed.

If you are looking for a carefully worked out system of answers to all your questions about life – you won't find it here. There is no lack of individuals and groups promoting a wide variety of such systems, but that is not the Unitarian way. What you may expect to find is some suggestions as to what tools may be most useful in producing at least provisional answers for yourself, not simply at the level of abstract thinking, but in the day-to-day process of living itself. Tools are intended to be worked with, and each one of us has a great deal of work to do. Life is not simple, and the reading of a book on themes such as those presented here, like the writing of it, means wrestling at times with knotty issues.

Again, if you are looking for the security offered in a group where everyone accepts the same beliefs, you won't find it here. Unitarians feel that they enjoy a deep and rich community life that does indeed offer them support, but it also offers them challenge. It questions as well as affirms; it demands personal authenticity rather than conformity. It requires of each of its members that they keep their eyes open, that they keep their minds open, that they keep their hearts open.

The present book is the product of a long evolution. In my earliest days in the Unitarian ministry, I was assistant minister at the church in Montreal. Angus Cameron, the senior minister, assigned me to lead a group studying what it means to be a Unitarian. I complained to him that I was unable to find a satisfactory book to use as background reading. Existing books were either out of date or aimed very specifically at either a British or an American readership. I wanted one with a more inclusive and contemporary approach. "Why don't you write it?" Angus shot back. So I did. I had originally wanted to call it *The Faith of a 20th-Century Unitarian*, but the publisher demurred, and it eventually appeared in 1955 as *An Unfettered Faith*. It evidently met a need, for two reprints were called for in the following few years.

But I myself was becoming increasingly unsatisfied with it. A colleague of mine, reviewing another book, said of it that it provided excellent answers to questions no one was any longer asking. Though I didn't think this applied to *An Unfettered Faith*, the rapidly changing context within which the perennial religious questions were being asked suggested that a different approach was needed. Implicit in the title, and to some extent in the text, had been the idea, traditional in Western thinking, that the paramount feature of a religion is its beliefs, usually expressed in creeds and dogmas, and that emancipation from these was the main feature of what I was proposing. Rather than taking this intellectualistic view of religion, I was now more and more emphasizing that it is a response of the whole person to the whole of life. So I wrote another book, and gave it the title *On Being a Unitarian*.

Once again, it appeared to be meeting a need. It went through four printings and was translated into German and, in part, into Hungarian. I was flattered by the number of people who told me that they had joined the Unitarians through reading my book. But another two

Preface

decades went by, and when another edition was needed, the world had changed again. I set out to make revisions, but they turned out to be so radical that what resulted was, as I put it at the time, a new book that plagiarized somewhat heavily from the old one.

This being so, again a new title was called for. This time I chose *The Unitarian Way*. The word "Way" has a long history in religious usage, particularly in Eastern traditions. It is the commonly used English translation of the Chinese *Tao*. The Unitarian Church of Vancouver, now producing literature in Chinese, is translating its name as what would literally be "Seekers of the Way," following here the example of the Hong Kong Unitarians. The word is also often to be found in Western traditions. It appears in numerous places in English translations of the Bible. A notable instance is the passage from the Book of Isaiah: "Your ears will hear these words behind you: 'This is the Way; follow it,'"[1] while the earliest Christians called themselves "followers of the Way."[2] Dante's great religious poem *The Divine Comedy* famously begins: "Midway on the journey through life ... I found that I had lost the way."

The Unitarian Way was first published thirty years ago. Time, with its inevitable changes, has moved on again. On a recent visit to England I was unfortunate enough to spend time in hospital, and during my convalescence at my sister's home in Dorset I took another look at her copy of the book. After this lapse of time it seemed almost like the work of another writer, but what impressed me was that despite all changes, it still seemed almost completely relevant to current conditions. I was bold enough to suggest to Lynn Hughes of Blackstone Editions, which published my more recent *Racovia*, telling the story of Unitarians in sixteenth-century Poland, that perhaps a new edition with minor revisions might be published. She shared my opinion of its contemporary relevance, and the result is this new edition.

To a considerable extent, any book of this kind must of necessity be a personal testament. But the intention is to present an approach that will command the support of most present-day Unitarians as well as giving a fair interpretation of the tradition in which they stand. One

---

[1] Isaiah 30:21.

[2] Acts 9:2, 24:14.

way of getting beyond personal idiosyncrasy is to use frequent quotation from others. This book uses many (some people might think too many) quotations; both from Unitarian and from other sources. They are included in the spirit of the words from the Book of Ecclesiastes: "The words of the wise are as goads, as nails driven home."[3] The words of others have often been driven home in my consciousness, and have certainly served as goads to my own thinking. They are not, of course, quoted as being in any sense authoritative beyond what you or I could have written instead.

Terminology can at times be controversial. I have maintained the international usage of the word *Unitarian* as the name of a tradition which has existed in many parts of the world for well over four centuries. However, American usage changed in 1961 when the American Unitarian Association joined with the Universalist Church of America to form the Unitarian Universalist Association. In subsequent years the term "Unitarian Universalist," abbreviated to "UU," came to be applied not only to the Association but also to individual persons. The Universalist movement had been almost entirely confined to the USA, so it did not seem appropriate to use the new American term when writing for a worldwide readership, to many of whom it would have little or no relevance or even meaning.

I am heavily indebted to the many with whom I have enjoyed the privilege of dialogue, particularly within the congregation of the Unitarian Church of Vancouver, where I served as minister for thirty-five years. I gratefully acknowledge the contribution of those who gave specific help, both in commenting on the earlier editions and in the process of layout and illustrations. Most recently, I am deeply appreciative of all the help I have received through the editing skills of Lynn Hughes.

Phillip Hewett

---

[3] Ecclesiastes 12:11.

THE UNITARIAN WAY

1

An Epoch of Homelessness

Current conditions around the world forcibly remind us of how precariously we journey into the future. Where are we really heading, you and I as individuals in our personal lives, and the human race of which we each form an infinitesimally small part? More and more of the familiar landmarks disappear, but are seldom replaced by anything we can wholeheartedly accept as better.

The scientific orthodoxy of the nineteenth century which provided a picture of the universe based upon mechanism and materialism has completely collapsed under the impact of quantum theory and relativity, though the full extent of this collapse is still not fully understood outside scientific circles, and the technological applications of the old point of view dog every step of our way. If a similarly complete collapse has not yet occurred in our economic, political and religious orthodoxies, it is not so much because we are generally happy with them as because the alternatives that were overidealized not so many years ago have all turned out to have very unwelcome features of their own.

Writing at the end of the Second World War, Martin Buber drew an illuminating distinction between what he called "epochs of habitation" and "epochs of homelessness." In the first, the human spirit "lives in the universe as in a house, as in a home." In the second, it "lives in the world as in an open field, and at times does not even have four pegs with which to set up a tent."[1]

For better or for worse, ours is an age of the latter kind. We may at times find this exhilarating, as we picture ourselves as pioneers exploring

---

[1] Martin Buber, *Between Man and Man* (Boston, 1955), 126.

new paths, in search of the new and the better. But we still look back as wistfully as pioneers have always done to the base from which they started and drew their supplies, with its warmth, its comparative security, and above all, its seeming stability within the natural and human setting that enabled one to call it "home."

In our present epoch of homelessness there can be no return to the ancient securities. We have been described as deracinated – cut off from our roots. In recent decades, millions of people have been uprooted against their will, forced by circumstances over which they had no control to leave their familiar setting and to reconcile themselves rapidly to new surroundings, new patterns of thought and behaviour. Millions more move voluntarily, and often continue to move at frequent intervals. Each such move means another breaking of personal and traditional ties, a further step away from the old settled order of things.

But the process is equally inevitable, though slower, for those who stay in the same place. The same place no longer remains the same. It rolls away from us even when we try to stand still. It is possible to become a stranger in the city in which one was born. The old landmarks we once used as guides are being swept away. The person who desperately wants to live by inherited traditions finds it increasingly impossible.

It is easier to come to terms with the inevitability of change than to derive much satisfaction from the directions it seems to be taking. No one welcomes the prospect of environmental collapse brought about by pollution and climate change. And the danger of a devastating nuclear war still lurks in the background, with the proliferation of possessors of the weaponry and the possibility of its acquisition by terrorists. We give endless time to debate over what to do, or indeed over whether we have enough effective control to enable us to do anything to modify the course of events at all.

Albert Schweitzer, who understood the nature and extent of the crisis far earlier than most, expressed his diagnosis and prescription in two striking metaphors. In his *Philosophy of Civilization*, published in 1923, he wrote: "Now come the facts to summon us to reflect. They tell us in terribly harsh language that a civilization which develops only on its material side, and not in corresponding measure in the sphere of the spirit, is like a ship with defective steering gear which gets out of control at a constantly accelerating pace, and thereby heads for catastrophe."[2] And how is the situation to be redeemed? Not by massive impersonal forces, Schweitzer believed, but by a return to serious reflection about the meaning of life on the part of individual persons, which would in turn bear fruit in action. "When in the spring the withered grey of the pastures gives place to green, this is due to the millions of young shoots which sprout up freshly from the old roots." The renewal of the world must begin in the same way with "a transformation of the opinions and ideals of the many brought about by individual and universal reflection about the meaning of life and of the world."[3]

If Schweitzer was correct, then this reaffirms individual responsibility in face of overwhelming forces seemingly beyond the control of any individual. If he was wrong, and the course of events is beyond redemption through any action of ours, the quest for meaning and significance on the part of each individual still remains valid, as in the days of the decline and fall of the Roman Empire. In order to live effectively at a personal level, we need to ask who we really are, and what place we hold in the whole scheme of things (if indeed it is realistic to speak of a scheme of things).

This search for understanding is an intellectual process. But it is far more than that. It involves us in every dimension of our being, and ultimately affects our entire way of life. It is a religious quest – though to use that terminology may be to invite instant suspicion and rejection from many people. Despite the perfunctory salute given in polite society to the importance of religion, it is generally regarded as in poor taste to admit to personal religious convictions and practices in the course of everyday conversation. Nothing is more likely to produce an embarrassed silence or an evasive witticism.

Reactions of that kind clearly indicate a high degree of disenchantment with what religion has been popularly supposed to mean. But to counterbalance this, there is also an increasing desire to break out of the conventional stereotype that produces such a reaction. That stereotype

---

[2] Albert Schweitzer, *Philosophy of Civilization*, vol. 2, *Civilization and Ethics* (1923; 3rd ed., London, 1946), 2.

[3] Albert Schweitzer, *Philosophy of Civilization*, vol. 1, *The Decay and Restoration of Civilization* (London, 1923), 101.

was satirized as long ago as the eighteenth century. In Fielding's novel *Tom Jones*, Parson Thwackum delivered himself of the classic comment: "When I mention religion, I mean the Christian religion; and not only the Christian religion, but the Protestant religion; and not only the Protestant religion, but the Church of England."[4]

Although Thwackum was a figure of fiction, he has his parallels in real life. T. T. à Beckett, a prominent Australian lawyer of the nineteenth century, fiercely defended the support of organized religion from public funds. But he responded indignantly when someone suggested that Jewish institutions should be among the proposed beneficiaries, declaring that he believed "no religion a religion except the Christian religion."[5] (His brother, by contrast, became one of the founders of the Unitarian church in Sydney).

Examples of the "Thwackum definition" could be multiplied. If we are to be realistic we have to acknowledge that the attitude expressed in this constricting caricature is still widespread in our own day, and influences popular thinking about religion more than we care to admit. None of us is immune. It is always difficult to get beyond a response, whether positive or negative, to the specific peculiarities of one familiar form of religion, and to come to see the universal features that all forms of religion share. An attempt to gain such a wider vision can again call upon words of Albert Schweitzer: "In religion, we try to find an answer to the elementary question with which each one of us is newly confronted every morning, namely, what meaning and what value is to be ascribed to our life? What am I in the world? What is my purpose in it? What may I hope for in this world?"[6]

Obviously there is nothing constricting or irrelevant in questions like these. But is this really what religion is all about? The nagging doubts persist. Isn't it about events supposed to have taken place in the distant past? Isn't it about what happens to you after you die? Isn't it about the things you ought not to do? Isn't it about coercing yourself and others into accepting prescribed and rigid beliefs, creeds, confessions of faith?

---

[4] Henry Fielding, *Tom Jones* 3.3.

[5] *Australian Dictionary of Biography*, 3:10.

[6] Albert Schweitzer, *Christianity and the Religions of the World* (London, 1923), 37.

An Epoch of Homelessness

All these characteristics, as well as others that could be listed, are to be found in particular forms of religion. Some of them are widespread, though not necessarily central, in many forms of religion. Parson Thwackum and his kin would gladly see us take any of them as a defining characteristic of religion as a whole. But religion as a universal reality in human life refuses to be confined within these inflexible limits. Schweitzer was right.

When we ask serious questions about life and about how we can live meaningfully and effectively, we are asking religious questions. In no way is this simply an intellectual exercise, like solving a crossword puzzle or a problem in chess. The basic religious questions are answered at the practical level through the process of living itself, and involve the whole of the personality, not solely or even primarily the intellect. Many people whose way of life shows that they have responded effectively to the challenge posed in the basic questions of religion would be quite incapable of formulating their answers into a philosophical statement.

Nor is the religious response simply an individual exercise. Since the dawn of history it has always drawn people into communities to question and reflect, to share and to celebrate. Religion transcends individuality. Answers to the questions as to what life is all about and how it is most meaningfully to be lived may be given in words or in actions, but in either case they can vary enormously. That is why there are so many different forms of religion, though some of them are not commonly identified as such. Within this wide variety of religious expression, there are some responses that are encountered every day by each one of us.

In the first place, there are people who are in complete despair over the prospects of improvement in their own lives, and often in the life of the world as well. The extreme form taken by this response is suicide. "What is there to live for?" Nor is this unhopeful view of the prospects of effective action confined to those who are conventionally called irreligious. Years ago I chanced to attend a church service in the Scottish highlands. Few sermons haunt the memory for that length of time, but this particular one does. Taking as his text "What shall I do to be saved?" the preacher dwelt at length upon various possible courses of action, only to conclude with the emphatic assertion that I can in fact do nothing, absolutely nothing. God will decide either to save me or not, and nothing I can do will make any difference either way.

A second, and not altogether unrelated, response to life's basic questions is that of "eat, drink and be merry, for tomorrow ... who knows?" Seize whatever fleeting pleasure the present can bring, and don't pause to count the cost. Life moves on from day to day and from year to year as a round of diversions and titillations, which effectively prevent the devotee of this creed from pausing to ask the fundamental questions as to what it is all about and why.

Very different is the response expressed in the call to return to the old truths and lifestyle which, we are told, we have recklessly abandoned. Starting from the obvious fact that we seem to be moving in some very undesirable directions, those who take this stance go on to argue that the only change of direction that is going to bring about any improvement is to retrace our steps. We need to return, like the prodigal in Jesus' parable, to the ancestral home, to the ways of life and thought imagined to have been typical of our ancestors at their best. We have gone hopelessly astray and need to recover our hold upon the ancient verities that we have foolishly abandoned. Back to the "old-time religion"! The trouble with this approach is that it is never possible to turn the clock back. No estimate of the present can be adequate which fails to recognize the advances that have been made as well as the mistakes into which we have blundered. The ancestral home is in any case no longer there, though some people may put a great deal of time and effort into trying to build what may at least give the appearance of being a facsimile.

Another avenue through which people have found meaning both in their personal lives and in the ongoing course of events lies in political action for what they see as human progress. In many cases they may be willing to go so far as to sacrifice their lives for the cause, whether that cause be nationalistic or ideological. Few descriptions of such a sense of meaning in service to a cause have been as powerful and frequently quoted as this one by the young novelist Nikolai Ostrovsky, an early devotee of Soviet Communism: "Man's dearest possession is life. It is given him to live but once, and he must live it so as to feel no torturing regrets for wasted years, never know the burning shame of a mean and petty past; so live that, dying, he might say: all my life, all my strength were given to the finest cause in the world – the fight for the liberation of mankind."[7]

By contrast, a quite different attitude commonly found among those in the industrial and military establishments of our day looks upon the failure of current procedures as simply a result of not applying them vigorously and wholeheartedly enough. Far from seeing any need to change direction or retreat to the past, they urge that we bring greater pressure to bear through a more forceful application of the technology we already have at our disposal. If the doors don't open at our touch, they can be battered down. Those who share this attitude tend to see religion either as a set of scruples standing in the way of effective action or as a bland set of mellifluous phrases that can be used to sanctify the status quo.

And then there are those who are vocal in their declaration that they have at last found the Answer; or at least, they have found someone who has found the Answer. Our age is replete with gurus whose disciples give them unquestioning acceptance, whose writings are taken as the last word on the Way, the Truth and the Life. These gurus come in endless variety. Some of them have unquestionably succeeded in discovering an approach to life that does yield meaning to themselves and to their followers, and bears fruit in a way of living that penetrates beneath the superficialities through which so many of our contemporaries skim. Others are charlatans exploiting the frantic search of increasing numbers of people for personal security in a chaotic world. Any of them who present their way as The Way cut off dialogue with the spiritual perceptions of others and enclose themselves within a sect. Recent history has given some dramatic illustrations of the dangers arising out of uncritical acceptance of any leader, no matter how initially plausible the person or the message.

These varied attempts to respond to the felt realities of contemporary life are all of them understandable. Within their own limitations, some of them may be commendable. But none of them is an adequate substitute for the process of reflection called for by Schweitzer. The person who begins with reflection, rather than with panic, fear, dog-

---

[7] Nikolai Ostrovsky, *How the Steel Was Tempered*, trans. R. Prokofieva.

matic pontifications, or blind acceptance of authority, can then proceed to effective action. This includes a sharing of many people's reflections, in a process that can issue in effective joint action. Here is the response proposed in the deeper forms of religion, though they differ in the degree to which they are prepared to consider the outcome of all honest reflection, no matter what that outcome may be. Within the Unitarian experiment there is a wholeheartedness in trying to accept the results of such reflection as completely as possible; without regard to whether the results appear to be traditional or novel, orthodox or unorthodox. Find out what you really think and feel, ask yourself in which direction you really want to move, share your reflections and intentions with others, compare them in dialogue, test them in practice. Modify them in the light of growing experience. Combine the power of growing convictions with an openness to the sudden insights that sometimes force a radical change of conviction. That, in brief, is the characteristically Unitarian approach to the problems, the possibilities and the perils of our time.

It cannot be emphasized too strongly that to become really effective, such a process demands a community within which to develop. Religious geniuses have, it is true, retreated from time to time into the forests or the desert to contemplate life as it were in the perspective of distance. But they have always felt the need to return to the marketplace, there to test their ideas and experiences, their aspirations and feelings against those of others, and also to gain the strength that arises from a supportive community.

The full dimensions of such a community become apparent when we realize that it extends not only through the present, but also embraces the past and the future, linking our lives as individuals with what has gone before and what is yet to come. The Unitarian community, never large in numbers but usually substantial in influence, has had a separate existence of its own for well over four centuries, though its antecedents go back through earlier traditions over a vastly longer period of time than that. In many ways it has played the role of what in other contexts has been called a "pilot project." It has brought together people who have shared a fundamental concern about life and its living but have been unwilling to bind themselves to dogmatic creeds and preconceived conclusions. It has undertaken an experiment to determine just

An Epoch of Homelessness

how effectively such people can work together in creating an effective community life that will foster the growth of personal insights as well as shared celebrations and endeavours. How possible is it for people who may disagree over details but accept the same broad principles to build a real "unity in diversity"? If such a pilot project is successful, then perhaps it may provide a microcosm of what is needed on a vastly larger scale, in a world where intolerance of diversity and unwillingness to consider alternatives to dogmatic conclusions may wipe us all from the face of the earth.

To some extent, the Unitarian movement has always been a pilot project. Many of the positions reached by Unitarians in the seventeenth, eighteenth and nineteenth centuries have been subsequently adopted by the larger religious bodies, with or without any acknowledgment of indebtedness to the Unitarian effort in pioneering. To give only one example, Unitarians of the sixteenth and seventeenth centuries entered into dialogue with Jews and Muslims on the basis that there were common religious concerns which transcended the fact that they themselves came from a Christian matrix. It was not until much later that the major Christian bodies came to accept a similar position. Even today, interfaith dialogue is suspect in many quarters. In fact, the more limited attempts at a rapprochement between the various divisions of Christianity often founder on the rock of an unwillingness to concede validity to the differing insights of others.

Communication between people of differing conviction and tradition involves an attempt to understand the real nature of the experiences and aspirations that are being conveyed through different vocabularies, or through different ways of using the same vocabulary. Even within an open tradition like the one maintained by Unitarians, the problem is enormous, which is perhaps why Unitarians devote so much time to talking about words. Ultimately, the most important aspects of life lie beyond being captured in a net of words, and there is often a contagion of spiritual awareness between those who do not even speak the same language. None the less, words are our primary form of communication. In such an enterprise in communication as writing a book like this, they are the only available form. It is therefore important to take a good look at the words we use, for they can mislead as well as lead.

This is particularly true when discussing the kind of issue that concerns us here, for this is an area in which we encounter peculiar difficulties in finding the right words. "Nothing holy ... admits of being defined," wrote the nineteenth-century Unitarian leader James Martineau.[8]

Such problems will be encountered again and again in the pages that follow. The popular travesties of what is meant by religion have already been illustrated, and this is only a beginning. The word "spiritual" is one of the key-words of religion, but many people have great difficulty in distinguishing the spiritual from the occult, spirituality from spiritualism. Similar difficulties attend words like eternity, myth, salvation and God, to which people commonly attach Thwackum definitions. How many are aware, to use another example, that "worship" is simply a contraction of worth-ship, and that the suffix "ship" denotes the cultivation of worth or value, just as "fellowship" denotes the cultivation of being fellows or comrades, or "scholarship" denotes the cultivation of being scholarly? To worship thus means to ascribe value, to celebrate it, and while for some people the highest value may be personified in the picture of a God in the form of an absolute monarch before whose throne one grovels and beseeches, to take this as the model of all worship is simply to accept a Thwackum definition. How many people's rejection of worship is based upon precisely such a process? And how often is the same true with regard to many other words in conventional or unconventional religious vocabularies?

Our problems with words are not confined to acceptance or rejection because of Thwackum definitions. Another frequently encountered peril is loss of meaning when words become detached from the life and thought that alone give them their value. They can become like coins that have passed from hand to hand so many times that their inscription has worn completely off. They slide easily across the surface of our consciousness in the form of platitudes which are indisputably true – in fact they are truisms – but have become so trite and commonplace that they have lost the impact upon our lives that alone can make them effective in practice. As Coleridge put it memorably in his *Aids to Reflection*:

---

[8] James Drummond, *The Life and Letters of James Martineau* (London, 1902), 1:154.

"Truths of all others the most awful and interesting are often considered as so true that they lose the power of truthfulness and lie bedridden in the dormitory of the soul, side by side with the most despised and exploded errors."[9]

Here is another reason for a failure of communication and a lack of effectiveness in action. The solution Coleridge proposed was this: "To restore a commonplace truth to its uncommon lustre, you need only translate it into action." To which it might be added that it can also be translated into fresher and more original forms of words. Translation is the key to effective dialogue, and to accept or reject any word without investigating what the user is really attempting to convey by it is to cut oneself off from the possibilities of fruitful communication.

---

[9] Samuel Taylor Coleridge, *Aids to Reflection* (London, 1872), 1.

2

Where Can We Look For Guidance?

What direction do we want to take in life? Whether or not we put such a question into words, our actions are giving an answer to it every day that passes. We move on from one point to another; life cannot stand still. The only question is that of direction, and of whether we feel that our free decision is making any significant difference to that direction. If we feel that it is not, then is this because the vessel's steering gear is defective? If so, can it be repaired or replaced? And then how do we decide which course we want to steer? Why do we want to follow that particular course rather than other possible alternatives? None of these questions is easy to handle.

In the "good old days" to which some people nostalgically look back, the issues were in fact simpler. During the Middle Ages, for example, there was a general consensus with regard to the course to be steered and why. Few people questioned the picture that was given of the purpose and goals of human life. It was the genius of Dante to give consummate artistic form to the consensus. His *Divine Comedy* had its roots in a form of society which, though remote from our own experience, was typical of those existing in most times and places. Each person had an accepted position and function in an apparently unchanging social order. Its traditional wisdom gave guidance as to how to think and how to live. To be sure, that wisdom was not always followed in practice by each individual, but those who failed to do so were prepared to acknowledge that they were transgressors. They did not generally call into question the validity of the rules and directions they had not followed.

Where Can We Look For Guidance?

This situation can exist only where there is a high degree of insulation from other forms of society which have different rules and directions. Such insulation has irrevocably disappeared from the world we now inhabit, even though totalitarian regimes in politics and religion may do their best to re-establish it in the areas they control. It may be prudent for those living under such a regime not to give open expression to too many questions, but inevitably the questions are being asked and are finding expression in one form or another. The demand for unquestioning acceptance of prescribed principles for all thinking and acting is continually being countered by the one word, "why?" If the reply is "because everyone knows that to be true!" then such a claim is too obviously false to be accepted by anyone aware of the wide variety of ideas and attitudes that actually exists.

One frequent response is to call in the experts. Here are people, we are told, who know a lot more than we do. It would be presumptuous to question their judgments. A great many people may in fact be happy to have such experts around, for it lets them off the hook in arriving at conclusions for themselves. Answers can be adopted ready-made from the experts, and this can often be defended as the reasonable course to follow. Who are you to question the conclusions of someone who has put a lifetime of training and work into a specialized field?

However, when dealing with the question of which direction to take in life and why, one is confronted with a rather different kind of subject-matter than when dealing with such a question as that of what load a bridge of given construction will safely carry, on which one could expect a fairly close consensus among competent engineers. In religion, who are the experts? There is no shortage of candidates for the position. They may sometimes be living persons. They may sometimes be persons no longer living. The expertise may sometimes be codified in traditions, books and institutions. It is not for you (we are told) to question what was said by the person, written in the book or proclaimed by the institution. It is enough that these are the words of Moses, or Jesus, or Confucius, that this was written in the Granth Sahib or Koran or Bible, that this is the doctrine of the Church.

The difficulty in maintaining such a position is that in every instance it is possible to ask why I should accept this particular authority, this expert, rather than that one. My earliest Unitarian mentor, G. Randall Jones, wrote many years ago in *The Religion behind the Religions*:

> In the Museum adjoining the Pump Room at Bath there is a glass case containing a miscellaneous collection of ancient Roman relics. Among them is a small metal tablet, with faint traces of an inscription on it. The attached card reads: "Incised inscription: read by Professor Sayce as a record of the cure of a Roman Lady by the Bath Waters, attested by three witnesses; read by Professor Zangermeister as a curse on a man for stealing a table cloth; by others as a curse on someone for stealing a Roman slave"...
>
> Here is a simple test of the expert's skill – the reading of an incised inscription. Professor Sayce was a front-rank expert in that particular branch of knowledge; he was one of England's foremost philologists, he served on the committee which revised the [English version of the] Old Testament, and his numerous works on the science of language are classics. But Professor Zangermeister was also an expert, and it is to be presumed that the others were acknowledged authorities. Yet they all read the inscription differently.[1]

What, asked Randall Jones, can the ordinary person do, lacking skills and information in this specialized field? An arbitrary decision in favour of one expert or the other would be meaningless. The only realistic course of action would be to say that the precise interpretation of the inscription is uncertain. But only a fool would infer from the differences of opinion that there was no inscription there.

Nowhere else (except perhaps in politics, where the immediate rules and directions of our social life are under review) is there as much disagreement among the experts as there is in religion. Not total disagreement, to be sure. No reputable religion argues that a life based upon hatred and spite is better than one based upon love, while in the deeper realms of direct religious experience there is a consensus of reporting behind the various terminologies used. But where it is a matter of theological belief, or of how to act in situations requiring moral decisions, the disagreements are profound. Nor is this the only problem in trusting the experts. In the nature of the case, no expert can live your life for you. It's your life and your decision. If you decide to follow one expert without question and to ignore all the others, this is still your decision.

---

[1] G. Randall Jones, *The Religion behind the Religions* (London, 1952), 19.

Where Can We Look For Guidance?

The more realistic approach is to accept that the responsibility is ultimately yours and to use the experts where they can be most useful. They can assemble the evidence and give their opinion, as in a court of law. But they don't deliver the final verdict. You, who have to live with the consequences, do that. You ask: does what this particular expert has to say bring out into an articulate form something that corresponds to what I feel, however dimly, within myself? Does what this person or book has to say open new and rewarding vistas for me, putting my own thinking and experience into a broader perspective? If I follow an "expert" because of this kind of response, I am not acting blindly. But if I am so overawed by the "authority" ascribed to the expert that I forget where the final responsibility rests, then I have abdicated my role as a person in my own right who has a unique life to live and unique decisions to make.

How do I discharge my responsibility most effectively? The first step is to immerse myself fully in all that is involved in making the ultimate decisions of life, the religious decisions. I use all the tools for responsible decision-making that lie at my disposal. For purposes of classification, these can be listed separately: reason, intuition, faith, conscience, and so forth – but it is important never to forget that these are simply names given to various aspects of what should in practice be the harmonious functioning of a total personality, in interaction with the whole of the environment without which it would not be what it is.

Recapitulating in his autobiography what he felt he had learned in the course of his long journey through life, the Unitarian philosopher L. P. Jacks wrote:

> It had been borne in upon me, more by the experience of life than by the study of books, that religion is the natural expression of ... the wholeness of human nature ... Given *wholeness* ... the growth of religion becomes spontaneous, natural and inevitable. But if, instead of wholeness, you have defect, arrest, distraction, distortion, disharmony (as when body works against mind or mind against body) then religion tends to wither, to die, to become a ghost, nor can you invent an argument that will restore it to fullness of life.[2]

---

[2] L. P. Jacks, *The Confession of an Octogenarian* (London, 1942), 198. Italics in original.

We need to remind ourselves constantly that the religious response which gives strength and direction to our lives is in fact a total response, and that any sacrifice of this wholeness means a fragmented personality. But at the same time, it is still possible to look at the various dimensions of this total response and to see how each reinforces the others. In attempting a classification of this kind, there is no universally accepted terminology available. The same name has been given to processes that are essentially quite different, while different names have been given to processes that are essentially the same. This whole field is a semantic swamp. None the less, its practical importance is such that an attempt must be made to work our way through it.

One word upon which heavy emphasis has traditionally been laid by the religion of our culture is "faith." Many people today (including many Unitarians) have difficulty in using that word, largely because it has so often been used to demand people's acceptance of ideas or procedures that put a heavy strain upon their credulity. One reaction to this is expressed in H. L. Mencken's definition of faith as "an illogical belief in the occurrence of the improbable."[3]

Any attempt to make faith simply a sub-species of belief is a Thwackum definition. In its broad historical usage, faith has stood for a process of active decision-making. It is marked, to be sure, by an absence of conclusive evidence:

> We have but faith: we cannot know;
> For knowledge is of things we see…[4]

See, that is, not only in the physical sense, but in the broader sense in which we "see" the solution of a problem after this has been presented to us in a logical argument. While the outcome of an exercise of faith, when interpreted in words, may look like a statement of belief, the more direct expression of faith comes not in words but in action:

> Columbus found a world, and had no chart,
> Save one that faith deciphered in the skies…[5]

---

[3] H. L. Mencken, "Types of Men: The Believer," in *Prejudices: Third Series* (New York, 1922).

[4] Tennyson, *In Memoriam*, prologue.

[5] G. Santayana, sonnet "O World, thou choosest not the better part."

Where Can We Look For Guidance?

If it is an over-simplification to reduce faith to an intellectual exercise (belief) it is equally so to reduce it to an expression of feeling (trust) or to an act of will (commitment). It is all of these, and they are inseparably fused in one response of a unified personality. The French philosopher Gabriel Marcel called it a "rallying to" whatever it is that one has faith in.

Faith becomes as important as it is in the process of decision-making simply because life is so indeterminate and unpredictable. Risk-taking is unavoidable in this world of uncertainties. Logical demonstration is seldom available, even in those fields where there is maximum effort to establish it. Alfred North Whitehead wrote in *Science and the Modern World*: "The faith in the order of nature which has made possible the growth of science is a particular example of a deeper faith. This faith cannot be justified by any inductive generalization. It springs from direct inspection of the nature of things as disclosed in our own immediate present experiences."[6]

Faith cannot properly be understood without its correlative, doubt. Both form part of one process and each is essential to the other. We live by both, and this is a fact that Unitarians have long recognized. It has been said that their patron saint is Doubting Thomas.[7] That may be a dramatic way of calling attention to a neglected virtue, but it really indicates no more than a shift of emphasis within the one process. To lay the stress here simply substitutes

> ... a life of doubt diversified by faith
> For one of faith diversified by doubt.
> We called the chess-board white, – we call it black.[8]

When is faith justified? One can point to the results, as in the scientific enterprise or the voyage of Columbus, but often enough the results are not yet available; perhaps they never will be. There may be attempts to explain faith in terms of unconscious mental processes

---

[6] A. N. Whitehead, *Science and the Modern World* (Cambridge, 1932), 23.

[7] See, for example, Gordon Donaldson, "Their Patron Saint is Doubting Thomas," *United Church Observer*, Toronto, April 1, 1960; Daniel Walker Howe, *The Unitarian Conscience* (Cambridge, MA, 1970), 83.

[8] Robert Browning, *Bishop Blougram's Apology*.

yielding insights that are not to be gained by the laborious piece-by-piece assembling of evidence in the search for demonstration. A distinguished American scientist, describing how this process works in scientific discovery, wrote: "Great working hypotheses have ... often originated in the minds of ... scientific pioneers as a result of mental processes that can best be described as 'inspired guess', 'intuitive hunch', or 'brilliant flash of imagination.'"[9] In the same vein, the French scientist Alexis Carrel said of such persons that "through intuition ... they unconsciously feel the presence of the unknown treasure ... A great scientist instinctively takes the path leading to the discovery. This phenomenon in former times was called inspiration."[10]

The processes of imagination and intuition here described are even more obviously characteristic of the artist's search than of the scientist's. Shelley, in his *Defence of Poetry*, exalted the power of imagination as "the principle of synthesis." Such powers of the mind are sometimes spoken of as non-rational or even irrational, but such a claim can be substantiated only by a Thwackum definition of "reason." One can endorse the seventeenth-century Unitarian philosopher John Locke's dictum that "faith, ... if it be regulated, as is our duty, cannot be afforded to anything but upon good reason,"[11] without subscribing to his very restrictive view of what constitutes reason.

Here is another word that has bedevilled discussion, though Unitarians have adopted it as the basis for effective decision-making for more than four centuries. One outcome of the narrow view of reason which sees it as consisting chiefly in verbal logic-chopping has been the accusation that adopting this as one's basis leads to an approach to life that is cold and calculating, or at best, very pedestrian.

Early in the nineteenth century the American Unitarian pioneer William Ellery Channing grappled with this question. "The term reason," he said, "is used with so much latitude that to fix its precise limits is not an easy task." But at least there is general agreement that it stands for

---

[9] James B. Conant, *The Overthrow of the Phlogiston Theory*, Harvard Case Histories in Experimental Science, Case 2 (Cambridge, MA, 1950), 5.

[10] Alexis Carrel, *Man the Unknown* (London, 1948), 120.

[11] John Locke, *Essay Concerning Human Understanding* 4.17.

Where Can We Look For Guidance?

"the highest faculty or energy of the mind." Among its functions, he went on, are two that stand out prominently. The first is "to discover universal truths, great and eternal principles...Reason is perpetually at work on the ideas furnished us by the senses, by consciousness, by memory, investing them with its own universality." The second of its functions "is akin to the first. Reason is the power which...is perpetually striving to reduce our various thoughts to unity and consistency. Its end and delight is harmony...It carries within itself an instinctive consciousness that all things which exist are intimately bound together; and it cannot rest until it has connected whatever we witness with the infinite whole."[12]

This emphasis upon unity and wholeness has repeatedly been seen as the hallmark of reason. Channing's English contemporary Samuel Taylor Coleridge defined reason as "that intuition of things which arises when we possess ourselves as one with the whole," opposing this to that mode of consciousness in which "we think of ourselves as separated beings, and place nature in antithesis to mind."[13]

Channing and Coleridge were doing no more than restating the meaning that the term reason has traditionally carried, though they themselves were living in an era like the one in which we live today, when the term was artificially narrowed to include only "the processes of logical reasoning, the deductive method of the geometrician, or the inductive methods of the experimental scientist, the historian and the detective."[14] In this restricted sense, reason would quite obviously not provide a satisfactory foundation for a religion, though the Unitarian emphasis upon reason has sometimes been so misconstrued not only by opponents but by adherents as well. Hence the repeated charge of coldness. Coleridge called it moonlight, that is, illumination without warmth. No doubt this would be a valid description of rationalism, which to many people would seem to have all the warmth and humanity of a computer. But to equate the Unitarian demand for rationality with trying to make a religion of rationalism is to play sleight of hand with

---

[12] *The Works of W. E. Channing* (Boston, 1883), 234-235.

[13] Samuel Taylor Coleridge, *The Friend: A Series of Essays*, Essay XI.

[14] W. G. de Burgh, *The Life of Reason* (London, 1949), 2.

words. There is as great a difference between rationality and rationalism as there is between spirituality and spiritualism, individuality and individualism, community and communism.

No one would wish to deny what Channing was quick to include in his definition, namely, that "reason is a calm and reflecting principle," but neither he nor his followers in the same tradition tried to pretend that this provided the sum total of the requirements for a satisfactory religion. As the leading English Unitarian James Martineau said a few years later, "To damp the fire down to the temperature of the fuel seems to offer but a small prospect of kindling anything."[15] Reason provides the fuel, but not the warmth. On the other hand, an injudicious choice of fuel may result in burning the house down.

The process of reasoning, properly understood, may then be regarded as an essential preliminary in religious decision-making. A great many others besides Unitarians would concur in that judgment. One of the best descriptions of the process was given by John Henry Newman, later a cardinal of the Roman Catholic Church:

> The mind ranges to and fro, and spreads out and advances forward with a quickness that has become a proverb, and a subtlety and versatility which baffle imagination. It passes on from point to point, gaining one by some indication, another on a probability, then availing itself of an association, then falling back on some received law; next seizing on testimony, then committing itself to some popular impression, or some inward instinct, or some obscure memory; and thus it makes progress not unlike the clamberer on a steep cliff who, by quick eye, prompt hand and firm foot ascends how he knows not himself, by personal endowments and by practice rather than by rule ... And such mainly is the way in which all ... commonly reason, — not by rule, but by an inward faculty ... The exercise of reason is a living spontaneous energy within us.[16]

He goes on to describe how, when we attempt to argue in support of the conclusions reached by such a process, then at that point we appeal to logical analysis. This may give rise to the mistaken impression that we

---

[15] James Martineau, *Hymns for the Christian Church and Home*, 8th ed. (London, 1851), viii.

[16] J. H. Newman, *Fifteen Sermons preached before the University of Oxford*, 3rd ed. (London, 1872), 257.

Where Can We Look For Guidance?

actually arrived at our conclusions through such analysis, whereas in fact it comes after the event, and may be beyond the capacity of many people who are highly skilled in the use of the process described by Newman.

It should scarcely be necessary to add that there is nothing infallible in any such procedure. Not every climber gets to the summit. Mistakes are not only possible, they are frequent. The idea of the infallible process, of total security, is a will o' the wisp. No one can claim immunity from the influence of forces that work below the level of consciousness to distort not only one's conclusions but even one's perceptions of the evidence. Depth psychology may have shed insights into the nature of such influences, but they have been well known to candid inquirers in all periods of history. A notable example may be found in the writings of Joseph Priestley, Unitarian minister, political reformer and scientist of the late eighteenth century, to whom the term "rationalist" may perhaps be more fairly applied than to any other leading figure in the Unitarian tradition.

Describing a critical scientific experiment in which he was engaged, Priestley wrote:

> When the decisive facts did at length obtrude themselves upon my notice, it was very slowly, and with great hesitation, that I yielded to the evidence of my senses. And yet, when I re-consider the matter, and compare my last discoveries... with the first, I see the closest and the easiest connexion in the world between them, so as to wonder that I should not have been led immediately from the one to the other. That this was not the case, I attribute to the force of prejudice, which, unknown to ourselves, biases not only our judgments, properly so called, but even the perceptions of our senses: for we may take a maxim so strongly for granted, that the plainest evidence of sense will not entirely change, and often hardly modify our persuasions; and the more ingenious a man is, the more effectually he is entangled in his errors; his ingenuity only helping him to deceive himself, by evading the force of truth.[17]

Priestley's own life-history gave additional and unintended weight to these observations. In spite of his clear understanding and statement

---

[17] Joseph Priestley, *Experiments and Observations on Different Kinds of Air*, 2nd ed. (1776). Reprinted in John A. Passmore (ed.), *Priestley's Writings on Philosophy, Science, and Politics* (New York, 1965), 139-140.

of the problem, he himself still clung to an obsolete theory that was invalidated by the facts he had discovered. Though he is known today as the discoverer of oxygen, he was incapable of making the mental switch required to acknowledge that this is what he had done.

Here is a salutary reminder of the limitations under which we all labour when trying to apply reason in practice. None the less, it still remains true that this is a more effective basis for responsible decision-making than such alternatives as blind acceptance of alleged authorities, or following the impulse and feeling of the moment.

When the issues to be worked on are moral dilemmas, the process is usually called by the name of conscience, rather than faith, reason or intuition. But the difference lies in the subject-matter to which the process is applied rather than in the nature of the process itself. Misperceptions of the evidence are more frequent in moral questions, as a result of unconscious influences arising from the requirements of parents in one's earliest years, or the traditional teachings of established authorities, or personal desires and inclinations. It is often much more difficult to liberate oneself from such influences when the question is "What ought I to do?" than in dealing with the kind of question faced by Priestley: "What ought I to think?" But the Unitarian stance has always been to ask whether there is a better way of answering such questions than the way of reason, and the inevitable answer is that of all available alternatives, this is the best one we have at our disposal.

Most forms of society display less willingness to tolerate what are regarded as eccentric opinions on matters of conduct than on matters of fact. A person who claims that the earth is flat is treated more indulgently than one who claims that it is our duty to rob the rich to help the poor. Aberrations of conscience are seen as more of a threat to society than aberrations of reason. The right of individuals to follow their own conscience was explicitly condemned in the Syllabus of Errors of Pope Pius X. This kind of reaction is only to be expected, for moral decisions result in actions that affect other people very directly. A limited recognition may be given to the rights of the conscientious objector, but this usually stops short of acknowledging that the objector's point of view might be the correct one. Although this can be seen as an oppressive restriction laid upon the individual, it has also to be recognized that the opposite extreme of toleration for whatever anyone may claim to be conscientious decision-making and conduct could lead to situations that no society could be expected to permit. Many of the terrorists whose atrocities have shocked our contemporary world have claimed to be following the call of conscience and the guidance of God.

Is there any acceptable procedure for distinguishing between reasoned judgments of an individual, on the one hand, and psychotic delusions on the other? The most promising course of action lies in bringing the best judgment of others to bear upon the same situation. "In the multitude of counsellors there is safety"[18] – but never infallibility. This is not a matter of abdicating one's own personal responsibility in favour of a submission to outside authority, but rather of entering into a fruitful dialogue in which one's own perceptions are tested against those of others in an atmosphere of openness and mutual trust. In this way, the map of reality that any of us plans to use for charting a course in life can be checked for reliability.

Ultimately, however, the responsibility still lies with the individual, a fact that is recognized by all systems of law when attributing blame or assessing punishments. Personal responsibility for one's own thinking and living is one of the central affirmations in the Unitarian approach to religious decision-making. It is precisely this affirmation that underlies the emphasis upon freedom that has been so marked a feature of Unitarian history.

---

[18] Proverbs 11:14.

3

The Charter of Freedom

Freedom! The concept wields an almost magical potency, whether expressed in this word or in one of the readily available synonyms: liberty, emancipation, liberation. The power of those under its spell to shake the foundations of the established order has been demonstrated time and again in the Western world ever since the Renaissance, and in more recent times it has girdled the globe. But in the process of becoming a popular slogan and ideological weapon, freedom has often lost its essential meaning. If what it really points to is a demand that individuals and voluntary groups be empowered to take on the responsibility for their own living and thinking without outside dictation, then the emphasis has often been laid far more heavily upon the demand than on the acceptance of responsibility. No doubt this has been inevitable, in view of the forces frequently marshalled against the freedom fighter, but it has had the result that for many who have enlisted in the struggle, the fascination lies in the chase rather than in the possession.

In a famous passage in his autobiography, John Stuart Mill, whose book *On Liberty* has become a classic, described the utter disillusionment that overwhelmed him when he forced himself to face the question of whether he would really be happy if all the causes to which he dedicated his life and work were to triumph. "An impressive self-consciousness directly answered, 'No.' At this my heart sank within me; the whole foundation on which my life was constructed fell down. All my happiness was to have been found in the continued pursuit of this end."[1]

Those who find the whole meaning of their lives bound up in liberation movements can rest assured that there is little likelihood of such

---

[1] J. S. Mill, *Autobiography*, chapter 5.

a consummation being realized in practice. If freedom appears to have been fully achieved in one field, there are always other, tougher, fields. The struggle, for some, moves from a fight against human oppression to one against natural evils, suffering, sin and even death itself.

How realistically can one assess what freedom or liberation means in practice? Attempts to grapple with this question usually point to two aspects of freedom, the first of them negative, the second positive.

In its negative aspect, freedom stands for the absence of something that is felt to be distinctly unwelcome. A person may joyfully claim freedom from oppression, or infection, or debt, or damnation. It would sound paradoxical in the extreme to make a similarly joyful claim to freedom from health, friends, solvency or salvation. But more than this, there has to be some serious possibility that the unwelcomed condition could in fact arise before we are likely to want to struggle for freedom from it, or to claim that we are already free of it. We don't usually congratulate ourselves on freedom from the possibility of being trampled to death by stampeding elephants, but we do congratulate ourselves on freedom from the possibility of being tortured to death by political or religious inquisitors.

In its positive aspect, freedom stands for the presence of something that we welcome, namely, the possibility of being able to realize more fully in practice what are felt to be our own highest potentialities, of making our own unique contribution in life, of working toward a life in harmony not only with our own essential nature, but with the nature of things as a whole.

Unitarians, throughout the more than four hundred years of their corporate existence, have worked incessantly to further the cause of freedom in all dimensions of life. In the first place, they have striven for an inner freedom that would emancipate the mind from bondage to prejudice and irrationality. Back in 1830, Channing declared: "Spiritual freedom is the attribute of a mind in which reason and conscience have begun to act, and which is free through its own energy ... I call that mind free which resists the bondage of habit, ... which forgets what is behind, listens for new and higher monitions of conscience, and rejoices to pour itself forth in fresh and higher exertions."[2]

---

[2] *The Works of W. E. Channing* (Boston, 1883), 173-174.

This particular dimension is one in which freedom is harder to secure than in any other. The influence of unconscious motivations, inherited presuppositions, fears and desires can never be completely eradicated or even fully recognized. Only a conscious attempt to steer by conscience and reason, with a constant checking of personal ideas and insights through dialogue with others, can produce the degree of liberation that would justify anyone in daring to adopt the name of freethinker. But such an inner freedom, once attained in any significant degree, gives strength and sustenance even in dark days when external freedoms have largely or completely gone.

The second dimension in which Unitarians have worked to establish freedom involves a throwing off of arbitrary constraints imposed from the outside upon the individual. "I call that mind free," said Channing, "which protects itself against the usurpations of society,… which respects itself too much to be the slave or tool of the many or the few."[3] Such a freedom is often associated with a democratic form of society, though this in itself provides no sure safeguard for individual freedoms. Socrates was put to death by a democracy. The tyranny of a majority over a dissenter may be as bad as the tyranny of an autocrat or despot. In fact, it may be worse, because it can be so much more difficult to dislodge.

Thirdly, a major Unitarian concern has been to establish and maintain free churches. By this is meant not only churches free of state control or interference, but churches which are free in their internal structure, so that no dogmatic demands are laid down as a condition of membership. The kind of free church worked for by Unitarians is one in which differences of honest opinion not only exist, but are able to interact in a fruitful dialogue. Such a congregation normally has a broad consensus on important matters, but almost everywhere there are dissenting minorities holding a different point of view and expressing it freely without embarrassment or bitterness. Sometimes a minority may represent a point of view that was once in the ascendancy but from which the main body of opinion has moved on. Sometimes it may constitute the vanguard of what will become the prevailing view of the next generation. Sometimes again, it may represent an experimental

---

[3] *Works of Channing*, 174.

point of view which will not stand the test of time and will eventually disappear. It is virtually impossible in any given situation to sort out exactly where specific groups or individuals belong within this classification. In fact, the classification itself is too neat to be totally accurate. But the important point is that the freedom of such varying points of view to co-exist and interact within the fellowship of the congregation is cherished and safeguarded.

The fourth area in which Unitarians have shown their determination to maintain and extend liberty is that of the state. An order of society in which basic human freedoms are upheld and respected provides the fertile soil for the exercise of a genuine freedom by individuals and smaller groups. Too often, however, the so-called freedom turns out in practice to be more nominal than real. Only a cultivation of freedom at more personal levels can enable the individual to see through and expose such shams. Unitarians have at times had to live under forms of society where respect for civil liberties was scant or non-existent. But they have always worked for the establishment of such liberties not only for themselves but for everyone. The traditional toast used at gatherings of English Unitarians in the eighteenth century was to "civil and religious liberty the world over."

All this is on the positive side. But in the excitement of conflict with those who try to restrict or abolish freedom, its defenders can sometimes lose all sense of perspective and go so far as to proclaim an unlimited freedom as the chief goal in life. A more sober consideration accepts that freedom is never unlimited. It always exists in tension with other positive goals to which those who value quality of life are also committed. The essential feature of freedom is the empowerment of individuals and voluntary groups to take responsibility for their own thinking and living. It is a means to an end, a part of a process, and the part cannot be taken for the whole without a complete loss of all sense of direction.

There is a certain arrogance in the unqualified claim, "I'm free!" As you look at the person who makes such a claim you begin to have your doubts. The freedom fighter who makes the revolution often succeeds only in substituting one bondage for another. That process is illustrated in the evolution of another word that is at root closely related to words like liberty, liberal and liberation, though less often used. That word is "libertine."

Originally, a libertine was someone who had once been a slave but had subsequently achieved freedom. Presumably, in a great many cases, the conduct of such persons demonstrated that a long experience of slavery was a very poor preparation for a responsible use of freedom once it had been gained. Later, the word libertine came to mean someone who laid claim to being a freethinker in religion, a person who insisted on coming to his or her own conclusions, which were usually quite unorthodox. In the final stage of its evolution – or devolution – the word came to be applied to someone who acknowledged no moral restraints, whose life was licentious and dissolute.

The route here traced is self-destructive. It leads directly to bondage, either deliberately self-chosen or brought inevitably into being through natural processes that have been set in motion. In the first case, there is disenchantment with the condition arising when freedom has been made the only goal and it seems to have been substantially attained. What does one do then? If all the fun was in the chase, how does one enjoy the possession? What ensues in practice is boredom and frustration:

> Me this unchartered freedom tires;
> I feel the weight of chance-desires;
> My hopes no more must change their name,
> I long for a repose that ever is the same.[4]

How many people have echoed this sentiment? What is the point of being free to go in any direction if you have no idea in which direction you want to go – if in fact you have no sense of direction at all? In the early years of the last century a book was published by the Catholic Truth Society in London telling the story of a man who left the Anglican church to become a Unitarian minister, with great enthusiasm for the freedom this would give him. Eventually, however, he became a Catholic priest. He is quoted as saying, as he made this latter move, "I have been wandering without star or pilot, and my head is weary, and my heart is filled with undefinable gloom." To escape this burden he sought the support of a system that could give direction and assurance. "Within

---

[4] Wordsworth, "Ode to Duty."

it," he said, "the individual moves, not as a meteor, but as a star in an order and activity, beneficent and divine."[5]

There have been, to be sure, some celebrated examples of Catholic priests moving in the opposite direction, to become Unitarian ministers. *From Authority to Freedom* was the title one of them gave to his autobiography.[6] But the rejection of freedom on the part of the man just quoted could be seen as grateful acceptance of a cure for a hangover resulting from the intoxication of unrealistic expectations. No one should ever suppose that the path of freedom is an easy one. Accepting responsibility for oneself does demand effort. The free is not the free-and-easy, though a great many people may still think so. From time to time one hears that being a Unitarian means that you can believe whatever you please and do whatever you like. The libertine is confused with the liberal.

Freedom is not an end in itself. Its substantial achievement in any area of life offers no assurance that its possessor is going to live happily ever after. Freedom is a means to the fulfilment of the unique potentialities for growth that lie within each one of us, but to use this opportunity effectively requires understanding and effort. George Santayana once remarked that freedom is like the air we breathe, necessary for existence but insufficient for nourishment. Those who expect to be nourished by it are bound to end up disenchanted, unless they come to realize that they have reached only the starting-point and have simply opened the way to taking the next step.

As against the irresponsibility shown in the caricatures, a responsible understanding of freedom acknowledges that it must always be in tension with constraints that are not only inescapable but (to use the Catholic word) beneficent. One such constraint is that of hard facts, insofar as the facts in any situation can be discovered. No one is free to believe that cabbages can grow from turnip seeds, if the constraint of hard facts is accepted in this way. Another way of putting this is to say that liberty is always limited by the demands of truth. The college

---

[5] George S. Hitchcock, *A Pilgrim of Eternity* (London, 1912), 11.

[6] L. P. Jacks, *From Authority to Freedom: The Spiritual Pilgrimage of Charles Hargrove* (London, 1920).

at which I was educated for the Unitarian ministry bore as its motto: "to freedom, to truth, to religion." The holding of freedom and truth in a creative tension is an essential characteristic of religion as here understood. From the New Testament comes the assertion: "You shall know the truth, and the truth shall make you free."[7] Knowledge is at the same time liberating and constraining – there lies the paradox. But it is not sufficient for nourishment. As Byron wrote:

> ... they who know the most
> Must mourn the deepest o'er the fatal truth,
> The Tree of Knowledge is not that of Life.[8]

It is not truth in the abstract that liberates and nourishes, but truth embodied and active as a powerful force in life. Response to this opens another crucially important dimension of responsibility: social responsibility. None of us is, in Donne's famous phrase, "an island, entire of itself." We are inescapably members one of another, and it is this fundamental fact that is ignored by the ultra-individualism that has often claimed exclusive rights in concern for freedom. Such individualism has succeeded only in producing the devastating sense of alienation and loneliness characteristic of so many people at the present time, and this in turn is driving them to take refuge in one form or other of authoritarianism.

This reaction when freedom becomes an end in itself, to the detriment of other claims upon us, is an old story in the history of religion and culture. In the early days of their existence, Christians made sweeping claims to liberation. "What Christ has done is to set us free!" wrote the Apostle Paul. "Stand firm then, and refuse to be tied to the yoke of slavery again."[9] That call found a ready audience. Many of them proceeded to use it as a pretext for every kind of irresponsible indulgence, and soon Paul and his successors were talking less about freedom and more about authority.[10] Before long, the rigid controls began which resulted in the totalitarian system of medieval Christianity.

---

[7] John 8:32.

[8] Byron, *Manfred* 1.10.

[9] Galatians 5:1.

[10] See, for instance, 1 Corinthians 5 and 6.

The same story repeated itself at the time of the Renaissance and Reformation. Once again, ancient authorities were to be cast off in the name of freedom. Once again, freedom ran riot into irresponsible licence on a wide enough scale to bring about a reaction to authoritarian controls.

The problem was that the enthusiasts heard only half the message. What Paul went on to say in the passage quoted above was: "You, my friends, were called to be free; only don't turn your freedom into licence and self-indulgence, but be servants to one another in love." [11] Literally, this can even be translated, "be slaves to one another in love." Is this then an ancient prototype for George Orwell's slogan, "freedom is slavery"? On the contrary, it is the product of deep and sustained reflection on the problem of how to distinguish freedom from its spurious substitutes. Paul was arguing that without love, liberty deteriorates into licence, and that love is an exacting taskmaster. Liberty and social responsibility are reconciled in love. Centuries later, Walt Whitman was to express the same idea in his own exuberant way:

> … Affection shall solve the problems of freedom yet,
> Those who love each other shall become invincible.[12]

As a matter of fact, this proposition is built into the historic meaning of the word "free." Its etymological root is in the old English word *freon*, which means "to love" and gives us the word "friend." This goes back originally to a Sanskrit word with the same meaning. The problem of freedom can be solved only in love. Love gives meaning and direction. But what is love?

---

[11] Galatians 5:13.

[12] Walt Whitman, "Over the Carnage Rose Prophetic a Voice."

4

The Reunion of the Separated

What does it mean to say that freedom is sustained and fulfilled only in love? How do abstract words like these translate into our everyday experience of life? The difference between the lifestyle of the liberal and that of the libertine is fortunately easier to recognize when you actually encounter it than it is to define in the ambiguous words at our disposal. The fundamental point here is simply that love is the response that ensures a responsible use of freedom. Centuries ago, the great Christian leader Saint Augustine put it pithily: "Love, and do as you will."[1] But unless we really understand what *love* is intended to mean, the message can easily be misread.

In popular usage, the word "love" has a whole welter of meanings. The English language lacks the terms possessed by some other languages to differentiate between them. For example, the Latin word used by Augustine in the phrase just quoted could not possibly be used for love in the sense of a tempestuous emotion: "falling in love." But this is what comes most readily to many people's minds when the word love is used. It was expressed very directly in a written response I once received after speaking on this theme from the pulpit: "What use is it to urge one to love? Love cannot be commanded or stirred up by the will. To me, love is a rare, deep, spontaneous emotion."

It would be absurd to deny that there is an emotional component in all forms of love. But to focus solely upon this makes it almost impossible to distinguish, on the one hand, between love and sentimentalism

---

[1] "Dilige, et quod vis fac." Augustine, *Ten tractates on the First Epistle of John* 7.8.

(which is the word used by those who want to brush any loving concern out of the path of their designs), or on the other hand between love and uninhibited desire, traditionally called lust (a word carefully avoided by those who want to present their designs as an expression of love).

The difference between lust and love is simply, in traditional religious language, the difference between using and enjoying. To quote Augustine again, "All human transgression consists in enjoying what we ought to use and using what we ought to enjoy."[2] Lust represents an attempt to bend things and people to what we conceive to be our own interests, without any regard for what they are in themselves. This is patently so in the sexual exploitation of another person, which often masquerades as love; it is also deeply embedded in much that passes for religious piety. Seven centuries ago, Meister Eckhart commented that there are many people who "love" God as they "love" their cow – for the milk and cheese and profit it brings them![3]

Nothing would be easier than to illustrate the decay of the meaning of love from the popular songs of the day – or, for that matter, from popular "inspirational" literature. Let it be sufficient to note that love is no gushing sentimentality or upsurge of emotion. Nor is it an attempt to use things or people. All these do no more than reflect back narcissistically the truncated illusion of the separated self. None of them establishes the genuine relationships that alone bring self-fulfilment.

Love is not so much to be talked about as to be lived. There are people who habitually substitute the first for the second, and assume that because they talk so much about love, they must therefore be loving persons. They then go on to argue that those who don't conform to the pattern they present must by definition be unloving. This is no more than a modern form of the traditional argument that those who don't accept the beliefs laid down in a particular confession of faith must be infidels, and its practical consequences can be just as devastating. With due regard to this peril, however, it is still necessary in the interests of full communication to talk about love as well as to practise it. For all the limitations of words, they are still indispensable tools, at

---

[2] "... fruendis uti velle, atque utendis frui." Augustine, *De diversis quaestionibus* 30.

[3] R. B. Blakney (trans.), *Meister Eckhart* (New York, 1941), 241.

least in the enterprise of writing and of reading in which we are here engaged.

In one phrase which goes to the heart of the matter, Paul Tillich described love as "the drive toward the reunion of the separated."[4] Here is a finger pointing the way. It indicates first of all that love does involve the whole person. It is not artificially restricted to what we conventionally call the emotions or the intellect or the will. It is a unified response. Secondly, it transcends the conventional individualistic idea of the self as a totally separate and autonomous entity. We find our fulfilment as selves only in relationship. Whether we are talking about love of God, or love of ideals such as truth and justice, love of the natural world within which our lives are set, love of the wider human community, love of our neighbour, love of close friends, sexual love between intimates – this one description covers all: the drive toward the reunion of the separated.

Erich Fromm struck the same note in his perceptive and widely-read book *The Art of Loving*. There he argued that the deepest of human needs is to overcome our sense of separation, to escape from the prison of aloneness, "to transcend one's own individual life and find at-one-ment."[5] There can be no doubt of this: here we have identified a fundamental need. And yet at the same time we find ourselves faced with a paradox. For even as we yearn to lose our loneliness in this greater unity, we also prize our selfhood, our own personality, our identity. Self-development, personal growth – these too appear as desirable goals in life for most of us, and we don't want to see them lost in a total disappearance of our personal identity with its own integrity. In fact, personal integrity has been one of the foremost of all values so far as Unitarians are concerned.

It is precisely here that Fromm showed his insight into these aspects of life and his understanding of the true significance of love. "Mature love," he wrote, "is union under the condition of preserving one's integrity, one's individuality."[6] Though love is an active power that breaks

---

[4] Paul Tillich, *The Dynamics of Faith* (New York, 1957), 112.

[5] Erich Fromm, *The Art of Loving* (London, 1962), 14.

[6] Fromm, *Art of Loving*, 21.

through the walls of separation, it still permits one to be oneself and to preserve personal integrity.

This co-existence within one total response of an awareness of one's union with a reality transcending the conventional limits of self, simultaneously with a reaffirmation of one's own personal integrity, gives meaning to the paradoxical words of Jesus: "Whoever seeks to save his life shall lose it, and whoever loses it will save it and live."[7] What is lost is the illusion of the encapsulated ego, the "life" that is translated "self" in other renderings of similar passages in the Gospels. What is saved, or discovered, is self-fulfilment through the very process of self-transcendence. The fundamental nature of love was further re-emphasized by Jesus (or, according to another account, by a lawyer in dialogue with him[8]) in the statement that all that is really required of us in life can be digested into two "great commandments": love God with all your heart and soul and mind, and love your neighbour as yourself.[9] This brief statement, which has been so frequently quoted but less frequently understood or put into practice, will repay a closer examination.

Setting aside for the moment the theological question of what we mean when we speak of God, a question which will have to be explored more fully in due course, we need to ask first of all what is meant by a commandment in this context. Can love be commanded? Not in the sense of being a response to the kind of command that a soldier is expected to obey. The way in which the word "commandment" is here being used corresponds to the way in which "law" is being used when we speak of laws of nature. What it means is that if a particular procedure is followed, then certain inevitable consequences ensue. The consequence in this case has been stated before the commandment: the question with which the discussion began concerned how to attain eternal life. Here once again the terminology can give rise to misunderstanding. Eternal life does not mean, as is often supposed, a life continuing in time for ever and ever after death, but rather quality of life that can be experienced in the here and now, and to which the passage of time is

---

[7] Luke 17:33.

[8] Luke 10:25.

[9] Matthew 22:36.

altogether irrelevant. It is what Alfred North Whitehead called "the vision of something which stands beyond, behind and within the passing flux of immediate things."[10] In Buddhist teaching it is called enlightenment. This is the essential goal of life and, said Jesus, it is to be attained through love as a total response of one's whole being: heart (feelings), soul (will) and mind (intellect).

Though love is an all-inclusive relationship, the two "great commandments" single out three dimensions in which it expresses itself. The easiest of these to understand, if not to practise, is love of one's neighbour, illustrated in the ensuing parable of the Good Samaritan. The love of oneself with which this has been directly coupled has been less generally understood. In fact, it has often been denounced as selfishness. Love of one's neighbour has been assumed to require mortification of the self. But this confusion has arisen only because we have allowed ourselves to accept a truncated view of the self as radically separated from the ecological web upon which it actually depends for its very existence. If we really come to understand the way in which relationships enter into the very essence of what it means to be a self, then it becomes a simple fact of experience that we cannot really promote our neighbour's good at the expense of our own, or vice versa. Love, understanding, respect for what really constitutes oneself is inseparable from the same response to the others with whom we are essentially united.

The third dimension of love, the most difficult of the three for many people to handle nowadays, was said by Jesus to be the greatest. That is the love of God. In very practical terms, what does it mean? Certainly it entails love of our fellow human beings, but if it meant no more than that in practice, then it could hardly be the greatest commandment. It would simply be a more ornamental way of restating the commandment to love one's neighbour. What it does entail at a practical level is a love, caring, respect, responsibility for what has traditionally been called "God's creation," a willingness to move in accordance with the rhythms of nature, a realization and a joyous celebration of the essential oneness of all things. "This is my body" can be said of the whole world, and the outward forms of behaviour that express this echo the inner consciousness that has been described in so many different terms in

---

[10] A. N. Whitehead, *Science and the Modern World* (Cambridge, 1932), 238.

the world's literature: "that serene and blessed mood" (as Wordsworth put it) in which we

> ... become a living soul
> While with an eye made quiet by the power
> Of harmony, and the deep power of joy
> We see into the life of things.[11]

This exploration of the insights of highly perceptive persons in both ancient and modern times into the essential nature of love takes us just about as far as words can go in indicating the nature of a response that is lived rather than talked about. In summary, love is a total response involving all aspects of our being; understanding and will as well as feeling. It lifts us out of imprisonment in the ego as a limited and self-contained entity into a liberation that relates us intimately to the ebb and flow of the various dimensions of our ecological setting. It shows itself in practice as what Schweitzer called "reverence for life," yet it includes more than we customarily think of under that heading, for it means also that we do not wantonly bulldoze our way through the majesty of mountain rocks or pollute waters remote from the haunts of humankind. Love implies an organic rather than a mechanistic approach to the universe that supports us in being, the kind of approach that has in fact been typical of most forms of society in the past and has thus far restricted the areas of the earth's surface that have been made desert by human agency.

One of the most apt words to describe the relationship involved in love is "intercourse." Although this has been narrowed in contemporary usage until it almost always connotes the purely sexual expression of love, it was traditionally used to describe all the varied aspects of the positive and reciprocal interaction between the self and its environment. In intercourse, fully understood, the being of the other is enjoyed and enhanced, not used and diminished.

Another word is "commitment." You are committed to whoever or whatever it is that you love. To quote Erich Fromm again, "It is a decision, it is a judgment, it is a promise."[12]

---

[11] Wordsworth, "Lines Composed above Tintern Abbey."

[12] Fromm, *Art of Loving*, 56.

The Unitarian Way

This emphasis upon love as the power that brings our lives together and makes the exercise of freedom responsible has been at the core of the Unitarian approach to religion throughout the period of the movement's existence. If it has seldom been emphasized in the very specific way it has been here, this is because the normal tendency in presentations of the Unitarian approach to religion has been to stress its distinctive characteristics rather than those it shares with all forms of religion that penetrate beneath the most superficial levels. If there is anything distinctive in the Unitarian approach, it is that the wholeness of its response is not compromised by conflicting and more exclusive claims. As Channing put it, "It does not weaken the energy of religious sentiment by dividing it among various objects. It collects and concentrates the soul; it gathers tribute from all regions and all ages; and attracts into itself all the rays of beauty, glory and joy in the material and spiritual creation."[13]

As a description of the foundation upon which religious community is built, this still sounds strange to many who have grown accustomed to the idea that acceptance into fellowship must depend upon the prior acceptance of shared beliefs, expressed typically in a creed. "What do you people believe?" is a question commonly confronted by Unitarians, no doubt because it is a question that can be immediately and directly answered by representatives of many religious persuasions. Unitarians have no recourse but to keep repeating that their community stands on an altogether different basis. Back in the year 1821 the English Unitarians composed a document which was written in Latin for general circulation in Europe. It contained the striking phrase, "they take love as their bond of union instead of faith."

It would hardly be possible to overstress the importance of this statement. For centuries it had been assumed that the bond of union in a church must be one of faith. The acceptance of a creed or confession of faith, affirming one's belief in specific propositions and doctrines, had been the condition upon which one could gain admission as a church member. With scarcely an exception, all the many new sects and denominations had maintained that principle rigidly.

---

[13] *The Works of W. E. Channing* (Boston, 1883), 387.

The Reunion of the Separated

Such a procedure might seem oddly at variance with the initial impetus giving rise to the Christian tradition of the Western world. Even the Apostle Paul, who had so much to say about the importance of faith, relegated it to a subordinate position. After describing the varieties of talent and personal contribution that individuals might bring to enrich the life of the religious community, he made it clear that the greatest of these contributions was love. Though most contributions had no more than a transient value, "there are three that last forever, faith, hope and love; but the greatest of these is love."[14]

But this has not been the official position of the organized churches. Faith has taken priority over love, and to make matters worse, faith has frequently been regarded as the equivalent of "correct" belief on matters of theological doctrine. Sometimes, in view of the difficulties often encountered in arriving at such belief, faith has been looked upon as having all the more merit because it has had to overcome a natural incredulity.

Faith, then, rather than love, was the generally accepted bond of union. John Calvin, the greatest of the early Protestant theologians, expressed it forcefully: "For the teaching of the Schoolmen, that love is prior to faith and hope, is mere madness; for it is faith alone that first engenders love in us."[15] Soundness in faith must precede the effective exercise of love. This ordering of priorities can be seen as the rationale for Calvin's action in having the early Unitarian Michael Servetus burned at the stake. So far as Calvin was concerned, Servetus was pernicious in his faith, and this was enough to outweigh any claims that might be put forward on behalf of love.

If, by contrast with this, love and not faith becomes the bond of union, there is no place for heresy-hunting and recriminations about differences in belief. Such differences provide a forum for discussion from which all parties may learn. The church becomes a shared enterprise in loving, an attempt to respond to others and to overcome isolation and alienation in a community seeking a responsible fulfilment of

---

[14] 1 Corinthians 13:13.

[15] Calvin, *Institutes of the Christian Religion* (1559), trans. Ford Lewis Battles (Philadelphia, 1960), 1:589.

freedom. In the words of a leading British Unitarian of the nineteenth century, John Hamilton Thom:

> Fellowship does not stand on the narrow basis of intellectual agreement. We maintain our spiritual fellowship in combination with absolute allegiance to our own individual convictions ... We will not suffer the one essential and universal attribute of spiritual love to injure the reverence for individual conviction which to the individual is an essential honesty; neither will we suffer our own individual conceptions of truth to separate us from the church, from the communion of any in whom that spiritual love exists.[16]

This remains an admirable statement of Unitarian goals. How often have they been realized in practice? The record, as always in such matters, is uneven. Individual Unitarians, like human beings generally, have run the whole gamut from love to lovelessness in their personal lives. There has been a similar, if not as wide, range among Unitarian congregations at various periods of their history. Ambition always outruns performance. None the less, the goal has always been kept in view, and there has been an impressive volume of testimony from outsiders who have seen Unitarians as contributing substantially to raising the quality of life for all.

---

[16] J. H. Thom, *A Minister of God* (London, 1901), 137.

5

Circles, Poles and Spheres

The most commonly accepted symbol for love, inclusiveness and wholeness takes the form of a circle. "Come into the circle of love and justice!" urged the liberal Jewish writer Israel Zangwill.[1] "Everything the power of the world does is done in a circle," said Chief Black Elk of the Oglala Sioux:[2] words that are frequently used in Unitarian marriage ceremonies with reference to the symbolism of the ring.

It is true that a quite different significance can be attached to such a symbol when those within the charmed circle attempt to draw a hard and fast line around its circumference to separate themselves from the unwashed who are shut outside. Yet even here the symbol itself is potent enough to overthrow such a perversion of its meaning:

> He drew a circle that shut me out –
> Heretic, rebel, a thing to flout.
> But Love and I had the wit to win:
> We drew a circle that took him in.[3]

A deeper insight into the meaning of the circle as a symbol of the power of love to build community comes when the emphasis is shifted from the line marking the circumference to the lines joining the innumerable points on the circumference to the one point of intersection at the centre. In his classic *I and Thou*, Martin Buber noted that while

---

[1] Israel Zangwill, epilogue to *Dreamers of the Ghetto* (1898). See *Singing the Living Tradition* #418.

[2] John G. Neihardt, *Black Elk Speaks* (1932).

[3] Edwin Markham, "Outwitted."

each position on the circumference may be occupied by an individual person, it is not the relationship of these persons to each other that creates the circle. "Not the periphery, not the community comes first, but the radii, the common relation to the centre. That alone assures the genuine existence of a community."[4]

This is a very ancient picture which recurs from time to time in religious literature. In the interpretation given by the seventh-century mystic Dorotheos of Gaza, the point of intersection at the centre is God. God is love. What the diagram illustrates so clearly is that the more closely we approach the centre, the more closely we approach each other, and conversely if we move in the opposite direction.

Another way in which this symbolism can be used is to look at the concentric circles that radiate outward from one's own life, which for any one of us is at least in some senses the central focus around which the world revolves. Each of these circles would include more than the one before, but within its own limitations each would also have its own wholeness and integrity.

The first would be drawn around the individual personality, safeguarding it against the pressures that tend to submerge it in the mass, but not forming so tight an enclosure as to create the illusion of total self-sufficiency.

At the second level, the circle would include a group in which all the members feel themselves related to each other as whole persons who can understand and support each other. Such a depth of relationship can of necessity embrace only a comparatively small number of people. Ideally, a family will form a group of this kind, although of course in practice many families do not. However this may be, the circle comprises a small group of intimates who are not drawn together by a specialized interest such as a common profession or hobby, but rather by an openness to each other as whole persons and a mutual willingness to communicate in those areas of life that are of the most all-encompassing significance and concern. These areas of life are by definition marked by a certain sacredness that renders them religious.

---

[4] Martin Buber, *I and Thou*, trans. Walter Kaufmann (New York, 1970), 163.

Circles, Poles and Spheres

The third circle is that of the explicitly religious fellowship, the congregation. This is normally a larger group, in which one participant does not necessarily know everyone else well, but feels none the less the contagion of a common spirit. Here is a group that gathers together regularly for the celebration and cultivation of deep insights into life, probings and questionings, shared consideration of the new ideas that are forever coming to birth in an ever-changing world. What is the real nature of the universe in which we are placed and what is our relationship to it? How are we related to one another, and what should be our attitude towards each other?

This circle is always open to newcomers, who are invited to share in the same enterprise. Inevitably the newcomer will need time to experience the full sense of community in such a group, born of familiarity not only with people, but also with their modes of thought and expression. The unifying spirit will not be felt by everyone with the same force. In any congregation there are people with all degrees of commitment. The boundaries are fluid, so that there are always those of whom it would be difficult to say whether they are really inside or outside the circle. Yet the way remains open for each person to gravitate towards the centre.

Beyond this circle lie wider ones again. Whatever the limitations of organizations and labels, it remains true that in all religious groups built upon this free basis there is a common spirit linking people together, which makes them able to communicate with each other on the assumption of a common approach to religion and life. Thus the Unitarian and liberal movement in religion, wherever in the world it may be found and under whatever label, has this common basis which will enable the traveller to recognize that it does form one circle, one community. Differences are many and obvious, but the underlying unity remains.

But the circles of inclusiveness cannot be limited by a similarity of approach to life's basic problems. A wider circle still has to be drawn, embracing all who have felt the impact of these problems and have tried in their own way to come to terms with them, though their way of doing so may have been very different from ours. This is the meaning of what is sometimes, but very inadequately, called religious tolerance. Basically, it is a recognition of the fact that when faced by life's ultimate majesty and mystery, each individual and group has to find an authentic mode of response, and that we need not quarrel with others because their response is quite different from our own.

Here is the basis of a real "unity in diversity," bringing people together in love despite the widest differences of thought and expression. Under such circumstances they can learn from each other and make a constructive rather than destructive use of their disagreements.

Early in the nineteenth century William Ellery Channing expressed his feeling of membership in a Church Universal in which everyone could share a sense of kinship with the great and good of all ages and places. "Do I not hold them dear? Does not their spirit, flowing through their writings and lives, penetrate my soul? Are they not a portion of my being? … And is it in the power of synod or conclave, or of all the ecclesiastical combinations on earth, to part me from them?"[5]

Yet once again such a circle cannot set the final limits to the inclusiveness of love. Beyond this circle uniting within itself all who are concerned with the basic issues of religion lies the circle of the entire human race, with all its diversities in sentiment, ideas and achievement in the art of living. In the fortunes of humanity as a whole we are all of us inextricably involved, even though with many of its activities and many of its representatives we may feel profoundly out of sympathy. But love is not contingent upon liking, and the parlous prospects for human survival in the world today re-emphasize as never before the need for a sense of community that shall not be based upon anything more limited than our common humanity.

Just as there is a danger in exclusive emphasis upon the smaller circles, so in the same way there are corresponding dangers in an exclusive emphasis upon the larger ones. We are all familiar with the phenomenon of the person who is so caught up in a love for humanity as a whole that he or she has no love available for those particular representatives of humanity who happen to live closest at hand. Wider loyalties build upon closer loyalties. They do not compete or conflict; they enhance and fulfil. But only in person-to-person encounter can real understanding, the foundation for sympathy, emerge. That is the unique and irreplaceable value of the small group. It is within the intimate setting that values are most likely

---

[5] *The Works of W. E. Channing* (Boston, 1883), 436.

to be translated into practice. Too heavy an emphasis upon the broader picture can cause one to lose the personal perspective and fall prey to the pernicious temptation to think that the individual may be sacrificed to "noble" purposes that are in fact no more than abstractions.

If the circle representing humanity as a whole should not distract our loyalties from the more limited ones, neither should it distract them from the wider one still. Our sense of fellowship should extend beyond the human race to embrace all that lives, in a deep-rooted "reverence for life." This gives expression to a sense of one's own participation in our entire natural and cosmic setting, recognizing that our life finds its ultimate fulfilment only as a part of the life of all that is. It may use the mystical language of oneness with God, or any of half a dozen other vocabularies. The form of words matters little; what does matter is a recognition of the oneness underlying the multiplicity which confronts us in the universe, and an acceptance of the fact that we are not detached spectators of this oneness, but inextricably part of it.

If there is any validity in this picture of ever-widening circles, then each circle broadens out from the one before it like ripples from a stone thrown into a lake. At each level there is an appropriate response to be called forth from the individual. All the circles range outward along our basic concern for life and its living, rather than the sectional and usually divisive interests represented by the circles more commonly drawn on the basis of race, nationality, ideology, class, wealth, skills or occupation. Too often circles of this sort artificially restrict our response and responsibility, rather than leading it outward more widely.

But we have not done with this metaphor yet. A circle is a symbol of unity and harmony; yet it should not be supposed that within any one of the circles that have been described there will be utter peace and tranquillity with no internal tensions and contradictions. Even within the smallest circle of all – that around the individual – this is not true. Much less is it true of the wider circles. They are maintained in being by internal tensions.

A tension can be constructive or destructive. It may be as constructive as that on the strings of a violin producing great music, or it may be as destructive as that on a rope which is about to snap.

One of the best pictorial representations of constructive tensions is given in the Chinese symbol of the *t'ai-chi*. This symbol is a circle divided in half by a line which is not straight but flowing, and shows expressively how the parts act one upon the other.

The two halves of the circle, known respectively as the *yin* and the *yang*, stand for opposites in tension with each other: light and darkness, heat and cold, male and female, good and evil, and so on indefinitely. They are held in this perpetual tension with each other by the surrounding circle representing the *t'ai-chi*, or ultimate reality. Destroy either of them and you destroy the *t'ai-chi*: you destroy life itself. The continuance of life depends upon the tension of opposites, though it should be added that no opposites are absolute. Each is arrived at by what is to some extent a process of over-simplification. The Chinese thinkers, in recognition of this, included a small part of the yin within the yang and a small part of the yang within the yin.

Such a picture of reality stands in marked contrast to the more usual one in the western world, where opposites must be engaged in conflict with the aim of totally destroying one or the other. This is summed up as clearly as anywhere in the picture of St. George and the Dragon. The struggle must end in total victory. The dragon must be slain. Sides must be taken in the battle; hatred for the enemy rules out an all-encompassing love.

Circles, Poles and Spheres

St. George and the Dragon

The consequence is a destructive conflict within the individual who tries to repress and exterminate the "bad" side of his or her personality. This conflict is often pictured as a war of the "spirit" against the "flesh." In the same way there is conflict between people – "the good guys and the bad guys," "the sheep and the goats"[6] – between races, nations and ideologies. Compromise is impossible, only total victory can be contemplated. From the personal level to the international, fearful destruction is the consequence, and to no avail, for after the destruction is over the "enemy" is still there. Far wiser is the traditional religious counsel to "love your enemies,"[7] whether those enemies are looked upon as human beings, or systems of ideas, or parts of your own individual make-up.

The symbol of the *t'ai-chi* recognizes this. It shows that the destruction of either of the opposites which confront each other must mean

---

[6] See Matthew 25:32-33.

[7] Matthew 5:44.

the destruction of the life that together they hold in being. But it shows also that the drawing of circles does not mean the elimination of all contradictions and tensions. Effective living consists in knowing how to handle these constructively, that is to say, in an atmosphere of love.

Suggestive though this circular imagery has been, it is still not the ultimate symbol of a rounded inclusiveness, for it is drawn on a flat surface and therefore remains two-dimensional. A further dimension is added if we begin thinking not simply of a circle, but of a sphere – a particularly significant image when one considers that we live on a sphere. Our planetary home is a globe spinning on its axis between two poles and divided by its equator into two hemispheres. The beauty of this picture has been brought dramatically to life in recent years in photographs of the earth taken from outer space.

The importance of this planetary symbol was brought home to me in discussions with Watson Thomson, perceptive thinker, social experimenter and long-time member of the Unitarian Church of Vancouver. In his book *Turning into Tomorrow* he wrote:

> The most significant image and symbol for our time is that of the globe – the sphere having roundedness yet containing opposite poles. Our planetary home is the symbol of the state of consciousness which will enable us to build that common house for the whole human family – twin poles and a round, containing sphere; polar opposites and the mind, of love

Circles, Poles and Spheres

and intelligence all compact, which can see the two poles together, and hold them together so that their conflict is absorbed into a larger unity.

We have seen now what is meant here by "wholeness" – the upright figure grasping and holding unflinchingly two opposite poles and circumferentially, a becoming-universal globe of human acceptance and belonging.[8]

There may be times when we need to grasp and hold unflinchingly in the sense of seizing both horns of our dilemmas. But then again, there is no need to hold on grimly, if one moves to the rhythm of an ultimate harmony that transcends polar opposites. To me this feeling is conveyed surpassingly by the symbol of the dancer, poised in grace and tension between an upward aspiration and the downward pull of gravity. She stands cast in bronze on a shoreline rock outside the little town of Budva in Montenegro.

---

[8] Watson Thomson, *Turning into Tomorrow* (New York, 1966), 36.

I place her against the planetary symbol as expressive of the creativity engendered by the tension between the poles. She dances. She moves gracefully within the tension, responding to the rhythms of the universe.

Hers is the cosmic dance pictured not only in religious mythologies but also in contemporary scientific theory. Fritjof Capra writes, "The whole universe is ... engaged in endless motion and activity; in a continual cosmic dance of energy ... Modern physics has ... revealed that every particle not only performs an energy dance, but also *is* an energy dance; a pulsating process of creation and destruction."[9]

An energy-dance is also expressed in the generally-accepted Unitarian symbol of the flaming chalice. It sets within a circle or sphere, a slender and very shallow chalice, from the centre of which soars a dancing flame. The almost cruciform design within the circle divides it not simply into two hemispheres, but into four quadrants, in the same way as the earth is divided not only into northern and southern hemispheres but also, more artificially, into eastern and western hemispheres by a division drawn along the plane of its axis. These four quadrants may yield various interpretations, among them that of the year divided into its four seasons.

---

[9] Fritjof Capra, *The Tao of Physics* (New York, 1977), 211, 232.

Circles, Poles and Spheres

The Flaming Chalice
To see this circle as a sphere might appear to be a forced interpretation, but it should be borne in mind that the chalice too is a three-dimensional form represented on a two-dimensional plane.

Symbols such as these are useful only to the extent that they can lead us toward insights that will be productive in our everyday living. However fascinating they may be in themselves, they are simply abstract toys unless, like the statue in Shakespeare's *Winter's Tale*, they can come to life and participate in our concrete existence. If they are able to do this, then they are not just figments of imagination, but the product of an intercourse between imagination and the world of experience. Century after century the basic polarities in life have enthralled reflective thinkers precisely because they have been felt to interpret the facts of everyday experience so meaningfully. One need only mention as examples the polarities between good and evil, freewill and determinism, life and death. Whether or not the encompassing sphere has been visible, the felt polarities have imposed themselves inescapably as quandaries to be wrestled with in one way or another. To look adequately at any one of them would require a volume in itself.

6

The Unitarian Dance

The tensions between a number of significant polarities have contributed to what may be seen as the distinctively Unitarian dance. Not that any of these tensions is experienced only by Unitarians. Anyone who attempts to live in a liberal spirit will be bound to feel them to a greater or lesser extent.

The first of these, frequently commented upon by outside observers of the Unitarian movement, is the tension between the head and the heart: between intellect and emotion, thinking and feeling, the rational and the romantic. As indicated earlier, Coleridge captured it imaginatively in the contrast between the moon and the stove. The moon gives light but no warmth. The stove gives warmth but no light.

Light is an ancient and worldwide religious symbol. In the Hindu Upanishads a story is told of a dialogue between a king and a sage in which the latter is being pressed to disclose the secret of enlightenment. What, asks the king, is the true source of light? He refuses to be contented when told in turn that it is the sun, the moon, the stars, the fire. The resources of the physical realm are eventually exhausted, and the persistent inquirer is rewarded by the discovery of the light that shines from within. But this enlightenment can be very differently conceived in Eastern and Western thinking. In the history of European culture it was the eighteenth-century Age of Reason that was known as the Enlightenment.

Warmth of heart, on the other hand, stands for something very different. A warm person is an ardent, caring person, someone who not only has feelings but is able to express them.

Neither the totally cold and unfeeling intellectual nor the warm generous individual who is totally devoid of any intellectual ability are persons one is likely to encounter in real life. Though they are caricatures, it has been generally assumed that Unitarians incline much more strongly to the former pole than to the latter. It would be unrealistic to deny that there are grounds for this supposition, notably in the statistics that show that the average educational level among Unitarians is far above the average for the population as a whole. This has given rise to the well-worn witticism that you don't have to be a Ph.D. to be a Unitarian – but it helps! Whether this is intended as a barb or a boast, it is still only a half-truth. The fact is that the Unitarian dance can be kept in motion only by the continuing influence of both poles.

The earliest period of the organized Unitarian movement, back in the sixteenth century, illustrates this very clearly. Its members achieved what the Polish historian Stanislas Kot has called a "synthesis of rationalism and love." The elements which entered into this synthesis were described thus by Earl Morse Wilbur in his *History of Unitarianism*:

> One group was found among those known as *Anabaptists*... Their following as a rule was among the humbler classes both intellectually and socially ... In temperament they were mystics ... and for the most part they had little interest in doctrinal theology. Their primary concern in religion was practical ...
>
> The other group was found among the Humanists south of the Alps. They were cultivated intellectuals of high social position and superior education ... In temperament they were rationalists, and their primary interest in religion was intellectual ... Religion was to them a system of philosophy, and the Church a school of definite and reasonable opinions.
>
> It will at once be imagined that if these two groups could in the course of time and by natural processes be somehow fused, a very interesting religious movement might result, and one stronger than either of its component parts. Such a fusion was in fact destined to take place in Poland.[1]

Like any broad historical generalization, this account of the genesis of the organized Unitarian movement is somewhat over-simplified. The two streams here identified were not totally separate; they flowed side by side in the lives of many individual pioneers before the emergence of an organized movement. However, it is equally instructive to note what happened to those parts of the original streams that did not merge in this way. The

---

[1] E. M. Wilbur, *A History of Unitarianism* (Cambridge, MA, 1945), 1:19-20.

Italian humanists who emigrated to Poland did so because intellectual integrity and therefore moral integrity became impossible for them in their homeland after the Inquisition established its authoritarian controls. Those who stayed in Italy were able to do so because their integrity meant less to them than their wealth and social position. They were intellectual dilettantes, and when the game became too dangerous they found other fields of thought in which they could be clever without being charged with heresy. Their intellectual systems were not really relevant to the way they lived their lives.

The Anabaptists who did not enter into this dialogue and merger were a much more numerous group. Most of them despised all forms of learning and relied enthusiastically upon first-hand direct experience. They attached a particularly high value to the visions and ecstatic inspirations which rapidly carried large numbers of them in the direction of an unbridled fanaticism. Several thousands of their most extreme representatives gathered in the city of Münster, divesting themselves of their property and, in some instances, of their clothes. To close any door was a crime, polygamy was introduced, and wilder and wilder utterances were accepted as inspired truths. In the end the town was besieged and captured by troops of the bishop, and the Anabaptists were slaughtered with frightful tortures. Less extreme elements of the same movement elsewhere organized themselves into communities where unquestioning obedience to the leaders became a way of life.

The perils into which people on both these extremes ran were avoided by the Unitarians through a sensitivity to the pull of both poles that enabled them to find the wholeness of response that Erich Fromm had in mind when he commented: "Reason flows from the blending of rational thought and feeling. If the two functions are torn apart, thinking deteriorates into schizoid intellectual activity, and feeling degenerates into neurotic life-damaging passions."[2]

There have certainly been times and places since that early period in which the Unitarian emphasis has become lopsided, and not always in the same direction, but on the whole Unitarians have usually managed to dance in the tension between the rational and the romantic, the head

---

[2] Erich Fromm, *The Revolution of Hope* (New York, 1968), 42.

and the heart. They have felt, to return to Coleridge's imagery, that neither the moon nor the stove could adequately meet their needs, and have sought the sunlight.

A second major example of the Unitarian dance in the tension between opposing poles is the one in which the demands of tolerance confront these of commitment. On the one hand lies the need for a sympathetic understanding of the varying codes and convictions that co-exist within a pluralistic form of society. On the other hand is the need to take a positive and definite stand in one's own personal life, and indeed in that of one's social group. Sometimes Unitarians have tried to evade the issue. Rumour has it that a Unitarian church once went so far as to display the slogan: "We believe in having no beliefs"! Such a spineless shirking of responsibility invites the classic retort that those who don't stand for something will fall for anything. There is a world of difference between committing oneself to definite convictions and committing oneself to fixed convictions. A compass needle points in a very definite direction while being in no way fixed; in fact, any attempt to fix it would immediately destroy its value as a guide.

Tolerance has been one of the traditional Unitarian virtues, and has been upheld at times within a very intolerant environment. During the seventeenth and eighteenth centuries it was pilloried by its opponents as "the Socinian heresy," after Faustus Socinus, the most outstanding of the early Unitarian pioneers in Europe. At that same period in history a ringing appeal for tolerance was issued by the Unitarian philosopher John Locke. Unitarians have always taken a stand in opposition to bigotry, fanaticism, intolerance and persecution, all of which, unhappily, are terms with strong religious associations. The word "fanatic" for instance, comes directly from the Latin *fanum,* meaning "temple." According to this etymological derivation, fanaticism was the frame of mind in which one was expected to come out of the temple. The French psychologist Gustave Le Bon went so far as to assert that "fanaticism and intolerance are the necessary accompaniments of the religious sentiment."[3] Unitarians have dedicated themselves to demonstrating

---

[3] Gustave Le Bon, *The Crowd: A Study of the Popular Mind* (New York, 1896), 64.

that this is simply not true, however frequently such manifestations may appear.

The frequency with which they occur does, however, illustrate very clearly the tautness of the tension between the open-mindedness characteristic of tolerance and the closed-mindedness so commonly associated with a commitment to firm convictions. Tolerance usually comes more easily in situations where one has no strong views of one's own, or where one's views have so little bearing upon everyday living that holding them is really no more than a game. Yet it is precisely here that one has passed beyond the point at which the term "tolerance" ceases to be appropriate. The proper word would now be "indifference," which stands in much the same relation to tolerance as the irresponsible licence of the libertine does to freedom. Of course the tension is going to disappear when nothing really matters, because there is no longer any pull toward the pole of commitment. But with its disappearance has also gone any genuine tolerance, which has to be grounded in difference, not indifference. Tolerance tries to understand and respect the differences between people. Indifference superciliously dismisses them as not worth considering.

The classic expression of tolerance comes in the words attributed to Voltaire: "I disapprove of what you say, but I will defend to the death your right to say it." Disagreement in such situations may extend far beyond what is said, and include also what is expressed in differing lifestyles, but a defence of the right of others to their own integrity is of the essence of tolerance. It insists that their integrity is entitled to the same respect as one would wish to claim for one's own.

In other words, the principle of tolerance is designed to serve the interests of people. Nothing hostile to the interests of people can legitimately be given our tolerance. Unfortunately, we don't always seem to be able to work this out very well in practice. We become so absorbed in the means that we lose sight of the end, or we become sentimental about the end and miscalculate the means. Often enough this can place us in a quandary. For instance, if one takes a firm stand on principle, one is liable to be called a cold, insensitive, unbending person who will follow a rigid course of action irrespective of the suffering this may inflict upon people, including oneself. If on the other hand one reacts against this and leans the other way, one is going to be accused of sacrificing principle to expediency whenever the going gets rough, of being completely unprincipled, of cowering to social pressures.

The only way out of such a quandary is to remember that the principle upon which one tries to act, whether that principle be love, or justice, or truthfulness, or tolerance, must arise out of and express a respect for persons. Those persons are not simply samples illustrating this or that principle. They are the ultimate justification for whatever principle one may accept as a standard in one's own life. Where they are being harmed rather than being served in the name of tolerance, there one is tolerating the intolerable. Here lie the limits to toleration, and it is an awareness of when such limits are reached that shows that one has standards.

To have standards is to take a stand, to make a commitment. It empowers one to grasp both horns of the dilemma, both tolerance and commitment. Raymond Holt, a Unitarian minister of the middle years of the twentieth century, coined the phrase "open-minded certainty" for the frame of mind this demands. Certainly there is as much of commitment in taking a stand for a truth you are humbly seeking as there is in taking a stand for a truth you arrogantly feel you possess. John Buchan, in his essay on the seventeenth-century Scottish military leader Montrose, who lived in "an age of violent contraries," declared in memorable words that "there is a moderation which is in itself a fire, where enthusiasm burns as fiercely for the whole truth as it commonly does for half-truths, where toleration becomes not a policy but an act of religion."[4] That is the kind of commitment sought by Unitarians.

A third major field within which polar opposites maintain a tension that is highly significant for Unitarians stretches between individuality and community – or as Paul Tillich described it in terms of the processes involved, individualization and participation.[5] One obvious feature of the evolving Unitarian movement is the extent to which its members have responded to the attraction of the first of these poles. They have always resisted being cast in a common mould and have insisted upon

---

[4] John Buchan, *Montrose* (London, 1938), 334.
[5] Paul Tillich, *Systematic Theology* (Chicago, 1951), 1:174.

making their own personal decisions. "Nothing is at last sacred but the integrity of your own mind,"[6] wrote Emerson, though in terms of present-day usage he would have said "personality" rather than "mind."

The line of development of Unitarian thinking on this subject was long dominated by the theories of John Locke. According to these, human societies were originally established through the voluntary surrender by free individuals of as much of their personal freedom of action as could be shown to be necessary for the setting up of a social order that would protect the rights of all. Beyond this minimum concession, personal autonomy would be preserved. Any organization, whether political or religious, which attempted to infringe upon this autonomy should be resisted. One is reminded of the citizen of one of the newly independent African states who returned his first income tax demand with the notation, "I did not request a membership in your organization, so I do not feel I owe you a subscription."

Research since Locke's day has shown his theory to have no historical basis whatsoever. In all forms of human society the individual was originally submerged in the group. Only at a relatively advanced stage in the evolution of the group does the individual emerge as a more or less independent personage. But the social contract doctrine long fascinated Unitarians. One reason for this was that it provided a justification for a high degree of personal freedom, as against the medieval totalitarian order from which Europe had so recently broken loose. A second reason was that although it did not correspond to what had actually happened in the earliest days of the human race, it did correspond to what had actually happened in the earliest days of the Unitarian movement. In various parts of Europe that movement began in the early sixteenth century with isolated individuals, and only after some years had passed did they get together in countries where organization seemed possible, to form groups and societies. Even after that, the feeling for personal independence ran so strongly that it often fractured the sphere representing the wholeness that alone can hold the opposing poles of individuality and community together within a constructive tension.

---

[6] R. W. Emerson, "Self-Reliance."

The Unitarian Dance

The result was that individualism tended to run rampant, and to bring alienation and loneliness in its train. Alienation depersonalizes those it infects: it is significant that *aliénisme* is the French word for insanity. When the ties of community are broken we become less than fully human, feeling with the damned in Sartre's *No Exit* that "hell is other people." One response may be a violent reaction against the individualism that brought such unwelcome results. Without the restraining influence of the now-broken sphere holding individuality and community in a creative tension, the victim may rush to the opposite extreme of collectivism, where closeness to others will indeed be found, but at the cost of sacrificing one's own individual integrity as a person.

Concern that the individualistic pull has been too powerful within the Unitarian movement has led some of its members into a sentimental idea of what constitutes community. This sees it as a cozy, nurturing environment dedicated entirely to mutual support. Here the focus is transferred from the centre of the sphere to the circumference. The line joining each individual around the circle is emphasized to the detriment of the line joining each individual to the centre.

There can be a narcissism of the group as well as of the individual, if it fails to realize that it finds its self-fulfilment only through relationship with its environment. Communities which have romantically ignored this fact have repeatedly and often rapidly collapsed. Where community has been maintained over long periods of time (as, for instance, in the monastic communities), it is because of a common focus that transcends the narrowly interpreted selfhood both of the individual and of the corporate body. An analysis of the successful *communautés de travail* established during recent years in France concluded, "Orientation toward a common task rather than toward community for community's sake ... in the final analysis saved the movement from complete disintegration ... When 'community' as an ideal takes precedence over the real things of our common life we are headed for trouble."[7]

The Hutterite communities, which have successfully survived four centuries, exercised for a while a powerful spell over the imagination of the Unitarians in sixteenth-century Poland. Gradually they came to

---

[7] D. B. Robertson (ed.), *Voluntary Associations* (Richmond, VA, 1966), 230.

realize that a closeness of this kind could not be effectively combined with the respect for individual differences that they cherished. But the attempt they subsequently made to combine individuality and community within a shared life was largely a failure.

The same has been true of other more recent Unitarian experiments in close community. They cannot be written off altogether, but if more success could be reported in this field, Unitarians would have made a significant contribution to one of the dilemmas facing free societies in all parts of the world. It would require a more explicit consciousness of the encircling sphere as well as of the polarities, and a more explicit repudiation of the individualism based upon the alleged self-sufficiency of an artificially circumscribed concept of the self. Preoccupation with this small encapsulated ego runs easily into the pathological condition of narcissism. Participation in a greater wholeness, on the other hand, can lead to a meaningful self-fulfilment. Martin Buber expressed the distinction succinctly in his *I and Thou*: "Egos appear by setting themselves apart from other egos. Persons appear by entering into relation to other persons."[8] Paul Tillich echoed the same insight: "There is no person without an encounter with other persons. Persons can grow only in the communion of personal encounter."[9]

Becoming a person in the full sense of that word means gaining a grasp of the wholeness embracing both individuality and community, and combining individual integrity with that full relationship with others that can be called communion and establishes community.

The Unitarian dance in the tension between individuality and community, between tolerance and conviction, between thinking and feeling, follows the same rules in each instance, as in many other instances that could be cited. Its success depends upon preserving the wholeness of the encircling sphere. If that wholeness is broken, then persons and institutions are torn apart. If it remains intact, then the dance can move in harmony with the rhythms of the universe.

---

[8] Martin Buber, *I and Thou*, trans. Walter Kaufmann (New York, 1970), 112.

[9] Tillich, *Systematic Theology*, 1:177.

7

Maps, Metaphors and Myths

The usefulness or otherwise of the symbolic pictures provided in Chapter 5 will have depended upon the degree to which they are felt to represent realities we know in direct experience, and to make it easier to deal with them in practice. The drawing of pictures in an attempt to do this is a normal part of everyday communication, but it can lead into endless problems if we ever forget that the pictures are representations of reality, not reality itself.

The confusion of the two has occurred with discouraging frequency not only in the history of religion, but in other fields of human concern as well. In science, for example, the dogmatism prevalent in the late nineteenth century was based upon the illusion that Newton's picture of the universe was something more than simply a model to help us understand the way things are. It was understood rather as a direct apprehension of reality, so that no alternative picture would be possible. If there is a greater degree of humility in scientific circles today, this is because none of the pictures now being drawn can even pretend to give a comprehensive portrayal and explanation of all known facts.

These symbolic pictures are like maps. Many different maps of the same area can be drawn, each designed for one specific purpose. Coastguards and mountain rescue teams can tell many stories of people who ran into serious trouble because they set out with nothing more appropriate than a road map of the area into which they ventured. When it is life itself that has to be mapped, the problems become far more complicated. What symbols will appear on our maps? What kind of symbols? They have to indicate not only which way to go, but what can nourish and support us along the way, as the maps of early explorers indicated where they could find food and water for their use, or wood for repairing their ships.

The realms into which we are now venturing are ones in which much depends upon intuition and imagination, and little can be proved beyond debate. Although most forms of religion have had their systematic theologians who have used logical arguments as their tools, the maps they have drawn have not proved as useful for most people as those drawn by the prophets, who drew heavily upon the insights of poetry, parable and allegory. The striking imagery used by the prophets made their words memorable and usable in a practical way that abstract argument seldom is. Such memorable utterances were passed down from generation to generation in ages when the art of writing was largely or completely unknown, and survived because people in each generation found them helpful in charting their own course in life.

In those earlier times, no one would have even understood the question that became important to so many people in more recent periods, the question as to whether the words of the prophet were to be taken as "true" in a literal sense. Metaphors were used naturally and unselfconsciously, as they are nowadays by poets. No one feels tempted to analyse the meaning of a poem by using the procedures appropriate to studying a treatise on logic or chemistry. We accept at once the depiction of a starlit sky as "all the firefolk sitting in the air"[1] without wanting to push the metaphor beyond the imaginative insight it brings to bear upon our more customary and more prosaic interpretation of reality.

Only through a complete failure of imagination can the characteristic language of religion be compressed into literal-minded interpretations that are expected to be as precise as algebra or formal logic. Metaphor is a fundamental feature of religious utterance, and its appropriateness is to be judged in the light of whether or not it assists us in finding our way and in living fully and deeply.

Various levels of imaginative language can be distinguished, shading off one into another. Beyond the simple metaphor lies the parable, which tells a story that in no way purports to describe an actual occurrence, but provides an insight into the nature of things or the way life should

---

[1] Gerard Manley Hopkins, "The Starlit Night."

be lived. Jesus made extensive use of parables in this way, ranging from slightly expanded metaphors (as in the parable of the mustard seed) to fully developed stories like that of the prodigal son.

Beyond the parable lies the allegory, a much longer and more detailed story in which the various participants and occurrences express symbolic meanings. Usually, if the allegory is successful, its meaning is self-evident to the hearer. Sometimes, however, an allegory or a parable has been deliberately used to convey in veiled terms a message that it would have been politically unwise to put into more straightforward language. The same is true of the kindred form of speech, the fable.

Allegories, parables and fables usually come from the creative genius of one person, who deliberately invents them. If they are successful, however, they resonate to themes deeply embedded in the subconscious lives of their hearers, having the same effect as metaphors that may not have been consciously devised, but well up naturally and spontaneously.

These forms of speech also assume that the word is to be the chief vehicle of communication. They suggest a circle of people sitting and listening to a speaker in a more or less passive way. But this is not the most usual way in which language has been used in a religious context. Just as music first arose as an accompaniment to action, and only later evolved into forms which required that people should sit quietly and listen, so also did the spoken word. Religious language was an accompaniment to rituals which required that everyone take an active role. These presented either a story with which the performers identified themselves, or else a desire for such things as rain or success in the hunt, enacted symbolically. Everyone felt involved, spectators as well as performers, and this religious ritual was intimately connected with the deepest concerns of everyday life.

This has been true in the same way of more recent periods in the development of religion in the western world. Dramatic presentations in which words were linked with the acting out of a story were performed in the churches of medieval Europe, sometimes as part of the regular services. In fact, the regular services in churches of a ritualistic type have the character of dramatic performances, in which the words spoken are not complete in themselves, but only as an accompaniment to action. And the action itself represents a story. It is usually a re-enactment of one of the central stories of the religious tradition, retold with the appropriate observances every year.

What exactly is the nature of these central stories of a religious tradition, built around persons and events rather than around precepts and principles? There has been much exploration of this question in recent years, leading into those realms where religions differ most strikingly from philosophies. In a word, this is the realm of mythology.

Here we encounter more problems in communication. The word "myth" is popularly used in a way that differs substantially from the way it is used in serious religious discussions. It has largely lost its connections with mythology in much the same way as the word "fabulous" has lost its connections with fable, but whereas "fabulous" has popularly come to mean "unbelievable but true," a myth has come to mean something that is believable (and in fact, widely believed) but false. The Shell Oil Company issued a series of pamphlets on energy conservation, one of which has paragraphs headed alternately *Myth* and *Fact*; another shows a picture of a dictionary alongside which is given what purports to be the definition of a myth: "purely fictitious narrative, person, thing or idea." In the same way the popular press refers to myths as needing to be "exploded" in the interests of understanding things as they really are. Even the religious press joins in; on the day when these words are being written, the current issue of a widely circulating religious weekly carries several references of the same kind in its editorial column.

Yet one is faced here with the same problem as in the case of other religious words that are popularly understood in ways that are narrower than or different from the ways they are used in serious religious discussion. There is no alternative way of speaking that carries the full force of the original word. One is obliged therefore to use a word that could be misunderstood, and to try to guard against this by explaining what one does mean. That there can be no guarantee of success in such an attempt is shown by the fury aroused in some circles when a group of thoughtful Christian writers, attempting to stimulate "the creative thinking which Christianity sorely needs today," ventured to call their book *The Myth of God Incarnate*.[2]

---

[2] John Hick (ed.), *The Myth of God Incarnate* (Philadelphia, 1977).

Maps, Metaphors and Myths

In its exact rather than its journalistic meaning, a myth is certainly a story. It can be told simply as such, which is the way most of us were introduced to the themes of Greek or Norse mythology. There may be instances in which the story is an elaboration of events which have an historical basis, though this is exceptional rather than usual. It is a product of human imagination, passed from generation to generation and evolving as it goes. The forces that produced and maintain it are deep-seated and powerful, for the story deals with issues that are momentous in the life of the community that preserves and retells it. Why are things as they are, either in the world as a whole or in the structure of this particular form of society? How did everything begin? How will it all end? Why do we suffer as we do? What does it mean to die? How do we find our direction as we journey through life, and how do we best equip ourselves for the journey? All these and other questions of the same kind are implicit both in the myths that have come down from the ancient past and in the ones that emerge even in such supposedly rationalistic times as our own. Both ancient and modern myths are retold and re-enacted as the calendar goes through its annual cycle and the appropriate season arrives once again. By participating in the hearing of the story and in its dramatic enactment, individual members of the community which shares such a myth gain a sense both of self-identity and of self-transcendence.

The myth that has touched the lives of all of us in one way or another, because it has moulded the evolution of the culture within which we live, is the governing myth of Christianity, the "myth of God incarnate." For centuries it provided the framework within which practically everyone's thinking and living took place, and though for many people today it may seem as remote as the ancient myths of Greece and Rome, it still continues to influence them in subtle and imperceptible ways. The way the Unitarian movement has evolved during the past four centuries is incomprehensible without taking account of the fact that it has been shaped in dialogue and debate with those who held fast to the traditional Christian myth, and what has thus been true of the Unitarian movement has also been true of all the other currents that have flowed in the life of Western culture.

The feeling of being adrift in an alien universe, so widespread at the present day, is in large measure a result of conscious or unconscious nostalgia for the old myth that so many have now abandoned. That nostalgia provides a ready audience for the multitude of campaigners calling for a return to acceptance of the traditional picture of the way things are.

That traditional picture, after going through a long evolution, had reached its fully articulated form by the late Middle Ages, say, by the time of Dante. Apart from minor modifications it remains the basis of the life of the Catholic church, the most powerful and representative force in Christendom. The account which follows is based upon the apologetic literature of that church. For those still able to immerse themselves in it, the traditional scheme gives the security of feeling themselves at home in a universe that is not indifferent to the human condition.

Though it points beyond the limitations of space and time, the myth proper begins with the beginning of time and ends with its ending. In the beginning, it tells, there existed one Eternal Being, perfect in every respect and beyond the power of human thought to comprehend. This Being may however be referred to by the masculine personal pronoun, "He." He existed alone, in a domain called Heaven, the realm of the skies. But though alone, he was not lonely. For not only was he one, he was also in a mysterious and incomprehensible way three, three Persons in one God, the Glorious and Blessed Trinity of Father, Son and Holy Spirit.

God, being perfection, needed nothing beyond himself. But as an act of divine will, or love, he began the process of creation by which other beings were called into existence. Vast multitudes of spiritual beings were created, lesser lights revolving around the Light of Lights and reflecting back his celestial glory. These beings were angels and archangels, cherubim and seraphim. Their function was to praise and glorify God, and subsequently, when other created things came into being, to serve as intermediaries between the pure spirituality of God and the grossness of the material universe.

Angels have freedom of action, but since they are pure spirit or thought they know all the consequences of their actions. Once they make a decision, there can be for them no change or repentance; neither can there be forgiveness, which is reserved for weaker and less spiritual creatures.

One of the angels was named Lucifer, or Satan. In spite of the impossibility of success, his inordinate pride in his own splendour drove him on to lead a revolt against God. Several million angels rallied to his cause, but the inevitable happened: they were defeated and banished from Heaven to a domain of their own, a place of torment called Hell. Satan's role was now that of the Devil.

At this point, therefore, the universe was divided into two parts, Heaven and Hell. But then God began further acts of creation. He created light, the realm of the sun, moon and stars. He created a firmament or atmosphere inhabited by the birds. He created great waters inhabited by fish. He created dry land, inhabited by plants, animals and at length by human beings, made by God in his own image. Like the animals, they were created in two sexes; the first man was called Adam and the first woman Eve. God set them in a garden where they lived in bliss, and gave them jurisdiction over the plants and animals of the earth. There was, however, one significant qualification. In the garden were two symbolic trees, the Tree of Everlasting Life and the Tree of the Knowledge of Good and Evil. They bore fruits which Adam and Eve were forbidden to eat. This prohibition, coming as it did before human knowledge of good and evil, was soon violated. Satan, pursuing his feud against God, approached Eve in the guise of a snake and urged her to eat the fruit of the Tree of Knowledge of Good and Evil. She was easily persuaded to do it, and in turn persuaded her husband. So occurred the first of the long series of human acts of disobedience to God, the technical name for which is sin. The sin of Adam and Eve was the Original Sin.

Sin brings punishment. God condemned Man (the Hebrew word "Adam" means "Man," so the two may be used interchangeably) to work for his living all his days; furthermore, he and Eve were to be exiled from the garden in case they ate also from the Tree of Everlasting Life. Pain and death, sin and evil, were to be the fate of all their descendants.

But God could not permit this temporary triumph of Satan to continue unchallenged. Though his justice made it necessary that the human race be punished, yet his love required that he find a way to bring them back to the bliss they had forfeited. To use the traditional terminology, God looked for a way to redeem them.

This did not follow immediately, though the passage of a few centuries can be no more than incidental to One of whom we are told that a thousand years in his sight are but as yesterday when it is past. To human eyes, however, the redemption seemed long delayed; things appeared to go from bad to worse, until at one time the primeval waters were summoned again to cover the earth and blot out human wickedness. But even the chosen few who survived the flood repeopled the earth with a race that was just as sinful as ever.

God's plan of redemption called for the coming upon earth of a Saviour. This Saviour would in fact be the Second Person of the Holy Trinity, the Son, taking human flesh from the stock of a chosen race, the Hebrews, singled out from among the peoples of the earth. For centuries before his coming this dramatic intervention by God was foretold by words and symbolic actions among the Hebrew people.

Then, at the predetermined time, the Saviour came. A virgin of the chosen race was impregnated by the Third Person of the Trinity, the Holy Spirit. Of this union the Saviour, both God and man, was born. He was the Second Adam, who would avenge the downfall of the First Adam at the hands of Satan.

The Saviour is identified with the figure of Jesus, but of the historical facts of the life of Jesus only the crucifixion plays any important part in the story. For the rest, Jesus of Nazareth and Christ the Saviour might as well be two separate beings, though they are inseparably fused in Christian thinking. It is Christ the Saviour who redeems the descendants of Adam from their predicament, by making a supreme sacrifice. Adam's Original Sin was an infinite offence: infinite because it was a direct affront to the infinite majesty of God. He and his seed could make no infinite restitution for this, which would be the only way of restoring the situation. But what they could not do, another could do on their behalf. The sin was, as it were, a debt; if the debtor could not repay, there was no injustice in someone else's paying it instead. The same procedure applies in criminal behaviour: if someone has been given the option of a fine or jail and has been unable to pay, it is quite permissible for someone else to pay the fine and release the prisoner. The traditional term for this is ransom, and in former times there were few crimes for which one could not be ransomed, if the sum offered were large enough.

The work of the Redeemer was to ransom the seed of Adam, to "pay the price of sin." This he did by submitting to death at the hands of the agents of Satan. But once he, an infinite and sinless being, had suffered death as the penalty for sin, the debt was paid, God's justice was vindicated, his love could prevail, he could manifest his power. The Saviour broke down the gates of Hell and redeemed all the righteous souls who had been imprisoned there during the centuries since the fall of Adam. Then, on the third day he rose again triumphantly to life on earth.

Now redemption is open to each and every member of the human race. All who identify themselves with the Saviour by an act of acceptance and faith may share in his victory. But those who do not accept him and identify themselves with him, eating his flesh and drinking his blood, remain under the power of Satan. The schemes of faith and ritual set forth by the various forms of Christianity simply represent means of identifying oneself with the saving power of Christ and therefore of rising with him to victory over death and evil. The Bible and the Church are agents in this process.

But it is impossible to be fully redeemed as long as one remains a physical being, for the fullness of redemption means admission to the presence of God in heaven, and heaven is a realm that can be entered only by spirits. Only after death can anyone enter into this state of bliss. For the redeemed, therefore, death becomes not a threat but the gateway to glory.

Those who are not redeemed, who do not identify themselves with the saving power of Christ, remain under the power of Satan, and their destination is Hell, the place of everlasting torture.

The end of the story is yet to come. There will dawn a day when God, who began the physical universe that we know, will bring it to an end. Christ, who according to some versions of the story was his agent in its creation, will be his agent in its destruction. He will return to earth on clouds of glory and separate humankind into two groups, those bound for Heaven and those bound for Hell. Then everything will return to the conditions existing before the creation of the sun, stars and earth, except that the redeemed among the descendants of Adam will be caught up into Heaven in the company of God and his angels, while the unredeemed spend eternity in Hell with the fallen angels and their leader Satan.

Such, in outline form, is the mythical picture of the ultimate meaning of things traditionally presented by Christianity. It is important to remember that this is not simply an exciting story to be told and listened to. All who tell or hear it participate in it; they themselves play the part of Adam, or Everyman. The alternatives of salvation and damnation lie before them. They are like actors in a play – in fact, the entire story can easily be set forth in acts and scenes like a Shakespearean tragedy. As in a great tragedy, the audience identifies with the actors and with the persons they portray; as in a great tragedy, the underlying theme is deep with meaning in terms of human experience.

As in a great tragedy, too, all the parts hang together. A few minor scenes may be modified or omitted, but cut out any of the major characters, such as the Devil or the Saviour, and the plot is destroyed. Some parts of the story could then be used in another drama, but it cannot be pretended that it is the same one.

The Protestant reformers of the sixteenth century, though they broke with Rome at many points, preserved the main outline of the drama intact, as the Orthodox Churches of the East had done when they split with Rome centuries earlier. But liberals of a later date, once they began to cut out major elements in the story, caused it to fall apart completely, though often they refused to recognize that this is what had happened. It is possible to build a religion around the figure of Jesus as a prophet and teacher who showed people how to live and taught them about a loving God who will preserve them from ultimate evil – but this is a far cry from Christianity as embodied in its historic forms.

Protestants as a whole, however, have throughout their history pushed the myth hard and far in a direction that was bound to hasten its decay. They treated it more and more as consisting of a set of propositions to be accepted intellectually, rather than as a drama to be lived in and acted out. By abolishing festivals and rituals in which the story was enacted, and limiting corporate religious observances largely to talk, they inevitably made the traditional story a more remote and theoretical

Maps, Metaphors and Myths

affair. At the same time they paved the way for Unitarians and other heretics, since what was proposed as a scheme of beliefs to be accepted at an intellectual level could also be rejected at an intellectual level.

This emphasis in Christianity did not begin with Protestantism, however. It had been there to some extent from the outset. While in other religions there was usually no attempt to anchor myths to history, there was a strong tendency in Christianity to assert that the myth did indeed give a factual historical account of real happenings. This could only work to undermine the true value of the myth as a piece of imaginative art, and to open the way for the weapons of historical criticism that were later to be applied with such devastating effect.

But this was not all. Alongside its myth, Christianity had always laid a heavy emphasis upon law. To some extent it inherited this from Jewish thought. In Judaism, as in some other religions, the system of laws and regulations by which people are to govern their conduct is seen as revealed and commanded by God. In the Jewish scriptures, from which Christians drew for part of their myth, there is frequent reference to a contract between the people and God. The people contract to obey God's laws; God in turn contracts to be their protector and send them prosperity. If one side of the contract is broken by the people's disobedience to the law, then God is released from his obligations.

Such a concept has the advantage of giving clear-cut standards of right and wrong, but the frame of mind it encourages is quite different from that in which one participates in the enactment of a myth. It encourages the temperament of the lawyer rather than that of the poet. It encourages a literalistic and logical approach to life rather than one of imaginative involvement.

In Christianity the idea of law takes a different emphasis. There was a widespread though by no means complete revolt against the Jewish interpretation of divine law as regulating conduct; instead, there arose an insistence that God had commanded not so much what we should do as what we should believe. Belief, not conduct, was to be prescribed by law. Just as under the older system God was thought to have prescribed penalties for those who didn't act rightly, so God was now thought to have prescribed penalties for those who didn't think rightly.

The result of this emphasis was that imaginative reflection about life's meaning and mystery, which gives rise to poetry and myth, was partially suppressed in the interests of a strictly disciplined intellectual exercise. The correct way to think was spelt out at great length, after the pattern of a legal system. Theology became the most important aspect of religion for those who accepted this emphasis, and this kind of theology became in large measure an attempt to present an intellectual interpretation of life in the guise of a code of law, much as Spinoza attempted to present his ethics in the guise of a system of geometry.

This tendency became more marked as the impress of Rome, with its traditional emphasis upon legal codification, was set upon Christianity, and it became almost all-pervasive in Protestantism after the Reformation. The two leading figures among the early Protestants, Martin Luther and John Calvin, had both studied law before turning to theology.

The result of this long process has been that for all Christians to some extent, and to many Christians almost entirely, religion became a matter of assent to the propositions which make up orthodox belief. Thinking outside the prescribed pattern was a crime. Often enough, heresy was regarded as a far worse crime than theft or assault or even murder. In fact, there have been times and places where these latter offences have been regarded as justifiable if the victim were a heretic.

During the most recent period, the picture has become much more encouraging. Though fundamentalist Christians may be as intransigent as ever, a strong trend has emerged within the mainstream churches to set the major emphasis upon religion as a way of meaningful living in a spirit of love and service. The classical myth, no longer frozen into over-literal interpretations, resumes its ancient power as the story within which those who call themselves brothers and sisters in Christ interpret and live their lives.

8

Inter-Religious Dialogue

The Europe into which the Unitarian movement was born was dominated by Christianity in one or another of its forms. The character of the newly-emerging movement could not fail, therefore, to be shaped, particularly in its earliest period, by the prevailing Christian myth. Dialogue between Unitarians and those who adhered to that myth was sometimes friendly, more often unfriendly, but agreement and disagreement alike required dealing with the same subject-matter, and inevitably the traditional Christian subject-matter provided the agenda. Since that time Unitarians have entered into many other dialogues that have shaped the evolution of their movement, but this was the first and for a long time the most influential.

The earliest Unitarians were all people whose upbringing had been shaped by the Christian myth. Throughout its history the movement has received a continuous influx of newcomers from the same background, bringing with them the influence of their earlier ways of life and thought and their later reaction against at least some parts of these. Moreover, Unitarianism has almost everywhere worked within forms of society in which Christianity has been the dominant religious influence. Naturally then, the ideas of Unitarians have for centuries been sharpened in dialogue with Christian myth and concepts.

For many of the early Unitarians the traditional scheme remained almost intact. They ventured at first to make only one or two further modifications to the structure, but the custodians of orthodoxy, both Catholic and Protestant, instinctively felt the danger to the whole edifice that the removal of these stones would entail. They resisted the Unitarians strenuously, using violent persecution against them wherever possible.

The Unitarian Way

The typical Unitarian response was to disclaim any intention to destroy the ancient edifice. They were, according to themselves, simply reformers engaged in the laudable task of removing those unnecessary accretions which were creating difficulties in the way of making it a habitable home. When they were denounced as heretical, unchristian infidels, they repudiated the charge. Not only were they Christians, they said, but they were the truest Christians. This line of argument has continued in some Unitarian circles almost to the present day. As recently as the mid-twentieth century, a prominent British Unitarian minister expressed it as follows: "In answer to the question, 'Do Unitarians regard themselves as Christians?' we may say: 'They ... not only claim to be Christians, but further, they assert that their kind of Christianity is Christianity in its simplest and most intelligible form.'"[1]

Arguments of this sort often appear where one form of religion develops historically out of another. No matter who has the best right to claim the name of "Christian," it must be obvious even at a casual glance that the Christian scheme of things outlined above and the typical outlook of a Unitarian have diverged further and further as time has gone by, and are today quite different. This divergence has been masked to some extent by the fact that many Unitarians have continued to use much the same vocabulary as traditional Christians, though they have used it to say different things. Moreover, in some places Unitarians continued for many years as members of the same churches as traditional Christians. There are countries where this is still true today.

In the English-speaking countries separate Unitarian movements developed during the eighteenth and nineteenth centuries, but before the break came Unitarians and orthodox Christians co-existed uneasily within the same churches. The same had been true for a very brief period in Poland in the sixteenth century. In England there were many Unitarians inside the established church during the closing years of the seventeenth century and for the greater part of the eighteenth. Men like John Locke and Sir Isaac Newton, who exerted a profound influence upon the whole of Unitarian history by their thinking, remained within the Church of England. So too did avowedly Unitarian contemporaries of

---

[1] G. Randall Jones in *The Inquirer*, 21 October 1946.

theirs like Stephen Nye and Thomas Firmin. In the eighteenth century so many members of the established church leaned towards Unitarianism that a petition was presented to Parliament to relieve them of the necessity of subscribing to the creeds. It was after this petition failed that Theophilus Lindsey withdrew in 1773 from his position as a clergyman of the Church of England and subsequently gathered the first avowedly Unitarian congregation in England. During the same period many of the Presbyterian congregations in England fell so completely under the sway of Unitarian thought that they eventually evolved into Unitarian congregations, the final stage being marked by the withdrawal of the remaining orthodox Christians. In America the same pattern repeated itself. Most of the early Unitarians were in the established church of Massachusetts, where their co-existence with orthodox Christians continued with increasing acrimony until the second decade of the nineteenth century, when most of the churches split, the larger section carrying the property with it. In other parts of the United States, Unitarians remained for years in the existing churches.

These historical facts masked the emergence of a new religion from the old. Unitarianism today is palpably quite different from what the overwhelming majority of people regard as Christianity, yet there are still Unitarians who claim not only that they are Christians, but that they are the truest Christians. And they can point to an unbroken line of descent from indisputably Christian origins. The mainstream of Christianity could conceivably have taken the direction they did, but in fact it did not.

The picture becomes clearer when we look at the way in which one religion does actually emerge out of another. A familiar example is the emergence of Christianity out of Judaism, where we see most of the same features. Christianity was indebted for a very great deal to Judaism, and some features of the Christian story, such as the Devil, the creation and the angels, come from Jewish sources. For some years after the emergence of Christianity a debate raged as to whether Christians were Jews or not. Most Jews said they were not, accusing them of abandoning important features of Judaism – the same sort of accusation as most Christians were later to level at Unitarians.

At this early period many Christians felt very strongly that they were indeed Jews and would remain so. This was the school of thought originally led by Peter, in Jerusalem. At the other extreme were some Christians who said they were most definitely not Jews – not only that, but they were bitterly anti-Jewish, repudiating any connection whatsoever between Christianity and Judaism and criticizing the character of the God worshipped by Jews. The leader of this school was named Marcion.

Between these two extremes lay the main body of developing Christian opinion, at first led by Paul, who declared that he would be a Jew or a Greek or anything else as long as he could convince people of the Christian scheme of things. Paul also anticipated the "Unitarians are the truest Christians" view in his "true Israel" theory: the Christians constituted the true inheritors of the Jewish tradition, while the Jews who did not accept Christianity (i.e., the overwhelming majority of Jews) had gone astray and were lost, though he held to the hope of their eventual redemption through their coming to an acceptance of the Christian interpretation of what their tradition really meant.[2]

But Christianity remained for many years in a state of more or less antagonistic dialogue with Judaism, just as Unitarianism has remained in a state of dialogue, more often than not antagonistic, with Christianity. For years the world at large regarded Christians as a heretical group of Jews, just as the world at large regarded Unitarians as a heretical group of Christians. As time went by Christianity entered into dialogues with other forces in the life of the world of its day which eventually became more important than the dialogue with Judaism: with the mystery religions of the Middle East, with Greek philosophy, with the Roman tendency to reduce ideas and forms of life to legal and ordered patterns. Throughout its history Christianity has absorbed the influence of the many forces in human life and thought with which it has come into contact. An outstanding example of this is the wide variety of elements from so many different religions and folk customs that have gone into the making of Christmas, which is at least ostensibly a Christian festival and has been interpreted by Christians in such a way as to make it so.

---

[2] See Romans, chapters 9-11.

Inter-Religious Dialogue

In the same way Unitarianism too has entered into a dialogue with non-Christian forces in life and thought which have had far-reaching effects upon its historical development and carried it further and further from Christianity as commonly understood.

Parallels must not be pressed too far. There are many striking similarities between the process by which Christianity emerged from Judaism and the process by which Unitarianism emerged from Christianity. But there are also two notable differences between the two processes.

In the first place, after its earliest period of all, Christianity developed in an environment that was not predominantly Jewish, but was dominated rather by the thought and practice of Greece and Rome. It therefore moved away from its Jewish antecedents more rapidly than Unitarianism has moved away from its Christian antecedents, for Unitarianism has developed in an environment the formal religious aspects of which have been dominated by Christianity.

In the second place, Christianity after its earliest period came to be backed by the political power of a great empire. It therefore grew rapidly in numbers and prestige, though the changes in its structure brought about by its rise to power were not necessarily for the better. Unitarianism, on the contrary, has not only not been backed by political power but has frequently been persecuted by political power, as Christianity was in its earliest days. No corresponding expansion, therefore, has taken place; the movement has remained small. This need not be regarded as necessarily a disadvantage. It means that those who have joined it have done so out of conviction rather than expediency.

One result of the great disparity in numbers and prestige between Unitarianism and the Christian orthodoxy with which it has been engaged in such a long and controversial dialogue is that Unitarianism has often had the appearance of being essentially negative in spirit. As more and more parts of the traditional Christian scheme of things came to be looked upon as incredible and unacceptable by a majority of Unitarians, so the movement was accused of being based upon denials. The most shocking denial of all was the denial of the deity of Christ and therefore of his pivotal place in the orthodox scheme of salvation. This was even more fundamental than the denial of the doctrine of the Trinity, which caused the defenders of Christian orthodoxy to dub the movement "Unitarian" back in the sixteenth century. For the doctrine of the Trinity is a somewhat remote and theoretical affair except insofar as it makes contact with human life through the nature, both human and divine, of its Second Person, and therefore becomes a logical consequence of the idea of the deity of Christ.

If the situation is looked at logically, it is at once obvious that to call a point of view positive or negative depends on which way you yourself are facing. You will call the views of those facing the same way as yourself positive and you will call the views of those facing the opposite way negative. Where two points of view are diametrically opposed, each can be presented as a denial of the other, and if they are not diametrically opposed, each can be presented as a denial of certain parts of the other. Unitarianism can be presented as involving a denial of the deity of Christ; Christian orthodoxy can be presented as involving a denial of the greatness of Jesus as a human being.

So much for the logic of the situation. But its psychology has to be considered as well. And here the weight of numbers becomes more significant. If a great majority of people accept one point of view and only a small minority accepts the opposing point of view, then the pressure is strong to regard the majority view as the positive one and the minority view as the negative one. The minority itself can be affected by this attitude, so that it can come to look upon itself as casting a negative vote. Many Unitarians have had the experience of catching themselves presenting Unitarianism as a rejection of the positions taken by Christian orthodoxy.

Much more serious is the situation which arises when the minority becomes so affected by a negative stance that it automatically rejects ideas held by orthodoxy simply because they are held by orthodoxy. As a Unitarian minister said years ago: "While there are good and sufficient reasons for disbelief, let us say, in the Virgin Birth, the orthodox Christian belief in it is hardly a reason for announcing that it is incredible."[3]

The fact that such an obvious statement needed to be made shows how much we are guided by the psychology rather than the logic of the situation. There is always a danger that the introduction of Christian terminology or ideas will so antagonize the Unitarian hearer as to bring

---

[3] Wallace W. Robbins in the *Christian Register*, February 1954.

about automatic rejection. The same holds true, of course, wherever dialogue becomes debate, no matter who the participants may be. And sometimes, under provocation from attacks by others, Unitarians have gone so far as to substitute satire for argument. Certain elements in the traditional Christian outlook have always been rejected by Unitarians: the exclusive claims, the cult of the personality of Jesus which went so far as to make a god of him, the low estimate of human nature and human effort.

None the less, although protest movements have their place in human history, it is ultimately on the basis of its positive contribution that a movement must be judged. If it becomes no more than a refugee camp from which the disenchanted attack the views they too at one time accepted, then it is simply parasitical upon the tradition against which it reacts. Unfortunately there are always people within the Unitarian movement who have become fixated at the negative stage of rejection, but at its best the movement has always recognized the positive values inherent in the Christian as in all other religious traditions, and has sought to draw upon these universal insights in developing its own distinctive approach.

There is another aspect to the whole question in which psychology becomes as important as logic. Unitarians shared from the outset in the almost exclusively intellectual approach to religion that is to be found among the early Protestants. It treated the Christian myth as essentially an intellectual scheme, embodied in creeds and dogmas which might be defended or attacked by logic. Two very disconcerting facts for anyone who takes this approach to religion have become more and more apparent over the years.

The first is that it is entirely possible to demolish a structure of beliefs by impeccable arguments and yet find its defenders not only unwilling to abandon it, but unwilling even to admit that anything significant has happened. For them this intellectual swordplay, though embarrassing, does not touch the vital core of religion. They hold fast to the myth, not as a set of logical propositions, but as a dramatic interpretation of life in which they participate and find meaning. As the story unfolds, it leads them to a feeling that they have resolved some of the most vexing and momentous problems of life and death. No wonder that something which can do this is not lightly abandoned.

To take a partial parallel from drama, the power over its audiences of Shakespeare's *Hamlet* is not in the least diminished by historical criticism to the effect that Hamlet was not really an historical personage, or if he was, did not do the things attributed to him in the play. Nor is it diminished by rationalistic attack upon the existence of ghosts. In just the same way the Christian myth can survive adverse historical judgments upon Adam and Eve, or the virgin birth of Christ, just as it can survive philosophical criticism of God or Satan. The power of the myth, like the power of the play, lies in the deep hold it has upon the emotions of the participants and audience, simply because it expresses and satisfies some of their deepest concerns about life and its meaning.

For those under the compelling power of the myth in this way, it will die only if it loses its hold over their hearts and lives. The intellectual contortions into which they are thrown in an attempt to defend themselves in argument do not disturb them very deeply; these are simply froth on the surface. The system to which they hold is not based upon history and philosophy, and cannot be dismantled by historical and philosophical criticism. It will be abandoned only if it seems no longer relevant to their life-experience.

The second disconcerting fact for the critic of traditional forms of Christianity is that those who do abandon them (and this includes a majority of the people in the traditionally "Christian countries" today) encounter surprising difficulties in finding anything satisfying to take their place. They often report a sense of loss and nostalgia for what they have left behind. This was poignantly expressed in the nineteenth century by the great biologist George John Romanes, who became one of the leading interpreters of Darwin's evolutionary theory. "The universe," he said, "has lost to me its soul of loveliness ... when at times I think, as think at times I must, of the appalling contrast between the hallowed glory of that creed which once was mine, and the lonely mystery of existence as now I find it, at such times I shall ever feel it impossible to avoid the sharpest pang of which my nature is susceptible."[4] He finally gave up the struggle and returned to the Catholic church of his upbringing.

---

[4] *The Life and Letters of George John Romanes* (London, 1896), 65.

Inter-Religious Dialogue

If such expressions of what is conventionally called "loss of faith" are less frequent today than they were for Romanes and his friends, it is because we belong to a generation that for the most part never knew at first hand the "hallowed glory" of the acceptance of the ancient myth, and has grown to accept "the lonely mystery of existence." Not that this makes our situation any more comfortable; frequently one hears expressions of envy for the unsophisticated faith of those who really entertain no doubts with regard to traditional religion. But though many voices are lifted up to urge us back to the old certainties, that way is forever barred to those who have drunk deeply of the spirit of the modern age. It would represent a form of intellectual crucifixion for which most people today are not ready, though they are surprisingly prone to fall prey to the specious myths of our time. In Nazi Germany, Albert Rosemberg's ideological book *The Myth of the Twentieth Century* became an influential best-seller. Its author was among those convicted of war crimes at the post-war Nuremberg trials and was subsequently hanged.

Whatever else it may prove, the widespread nostalgia for the abandoned myths of our past and the equally widespread readiness to accept the no less illogical myths of the present show that we do not live by intellect alone. The vacuum created by the decline of traditional religion has to be replaced not only at the level of thought – that is comparatively easy – but also at the level of feeling. This is a lesson that Unitarians are beginning to absorb. It is now possible to draw inspiration from all the world's myths without being possessed by any of them. When they are treated in this way, it becomes apparent that there are deep psychological truths portrayed in all of them, which can be portrayed also in modern poetry, drama and art. These too can be brought into the service of the church, as a new and exciting era of discovery begins. We may be, as Buber asserted, in an epoch of homelessness, but this too can be celebrated in song and story, and warmed by the fire of love.

Now that mainstream Christian churches are showing so many more signs of willingness to enter into a broader religious dialogue, the long history of Unitarian relationships with the tradition they represent may be expected to continue in a more positive and fruitful way than has often been true in the past. Those relationships have been supplemented in recent years by a growing dialogue with other world religions, as their life and thought have become increasingly accessible to those raised within a Western culture. Back in the sixteenth and seventeenth centuries, the only non-Christian religions in any way accessible to the early Unitarians were Judaism and Islam, but there were attempts none the less to enter into significant discussions, particularly with members of the Jewish communities of eastern Europe.

In more recent times, dialogue with Judaism has been frequent and fruitful, the more so because substantial numbers of Unitarians have come into the movement from a Jewish rather than a Christian background. They have had to cope in the same way with the tension between nostalgia and rejection, and to find their own way of resolving it. But Unitarians whose background has been Christian rather than Jewish have made significant contributions to building more positive relations between the two historic religions of the West. For instance, it was a Unitarian scholar, Travers Herford, who early in the last century was the first non-Jew to demonstrate by painstaking research just how one-sided and unfair was the picture of the Pharisees that has been handed down in the Christian tradition.[5]

As early as 1682 there was an attempt to broaden the discussion to include Islam, when some English Unitarians made an unsuccessful effort to get in touch with the Moroccan ambassador in London to discuss their respective religious positions. When in the nineteenth century the opportunity came to enter with some degree of understanding into the thought-world of the Orient, leading Unitarians seized it eagerly, and one of them in particular, Estlin Carpenter, made a lasting contribution to the new study of comparative religion. They were in agreement with Max Müller (who spoke many times under Unitarian auspices) when he said that a person who knows only one religion knows none.[6] Only by testing our ideas in a free atmosphere against those of people who think in ways very different from our own can we really come to grips with those presuppositions of our point of view which we too easily take for granted.

---

[5] R. Travers Herford, *The Pharisees* (London, 1924).

[6] Max Müller, *Introduction to the Science of Religion* (London, 1873), 12.

Inter-Religious Dialogue

Religions have been aptly compared to languages. They represent different ways of trying to report on and interpret some fundamental and universal facts of human experience. There are still hostilities between people because they speak different languages. Language as such is a means of communication; the existence of so many different languages forms a barrier to communication. Exact translation from one language to another is sometimes impossible, because the language itself forms part of the interpretation of the experience described.

All these features are true of the various religions too. They crystallize basic responses to life in certain generally accepted forms which not only report experiences but also interpret them. Each tradition has its own vocabulary both of words and of patterns of thought. When different traditions confront each other, the important matter is not to quarrel about the vocabularies used but to uncover what they are attempting to convey. This, however, is seldom done. We content ourselves with a war of words.

The developing Unitarian dialogue with the various traditions of world religion opens up new possibilities of enormous significance. First, it re-emphasizes that words and symbols are of value only to the extent that they convey real meanings, and that the same meanings may be conveyed through various words and symbols. The attempt to translate from one to another can broaden our outlook immeasurably.

Second, it exposes the need for some understanding and mutual acceptance between the various traditions of world religion. It is tragic that at a time when the dangers of conflict are so great and the need for ways of bringing people together is so desperate, organized religion is in so poor a position to furnish leadership in promoting world unity. Instead, religion is more often a force for producing divisions rather than for bringing people together. Although the political leaders of the world can at least sit down in a common debating hall, the same has not been true of religious leaders. The nearest parallel has been the Parliament of the World's Religions, with a number of sessions in recent years, but it has been composed of individual registrants rather than leaders wielding organizational influence. In this and other interfaith bodies Unitarians have continued to work for understanding and cooperation.

9

The Spirit of the Age

The dialogues shaping the evolution of the Unitarian movement have by no means been solely with representatives of the various religious traditions. If that had been so, the movement would have been largely isolated from the vital forces shaping the life of the modern age, amongst which organized religion does not loom large. Unless there is continuing communication in terms of mutual respect and some degree of understanding with the formative influences in human life in each generation, a religious body lapses into sectarian isolation. Unitarians have always rejected the idea of retreat into a ghetto. Throughout their history they have attempted to engage in creative intercourse with the forces shaping the life of the world.

The revolutionary force shaking up the whole life of Europe in the period immediately preceding the birth of the Unitarian movement was that of the Renaissance. This spectacular upheaval in human consciousness brought the medieval era to a close and ushered in the modern age. It re-evaluated the past by taking a new look at the positive achievements of the human spirit in the science, art and philosophy of the classical period preceding the Dark Ages. In its later and more productive phase it began anew where the ancient world had left off, and with the aid of new attitudes and techniques began to build its own science, philosophy and art. Again, there was optimism rather than pessimism with regard to the possibilities of accomplishment through human effort. The more extreme of the Renaissance thinkers set no limits to such possibilities; even the more modest among their number were humanists in the sense that their dominant focus was upon human interests and human accomplishment.

The Spirit of the Age

The Renaissance began and flowered most luxuriantly in Italy. It is no accident that this is also where Unitarian ideas began first to germinate. If one looks at the names of those who in the middle of the sixteenth century were feeling their way towards a Unitarian position and were to set the Unitarian movement in motion, one sees how overwhelmingly Italian the influence was. This stood in marked contrast with the Protestant reformation, where most of the leaders were drawn from the northern half of Europe.

With the exception of Servetus and Valdés, who were Spaniards, Castellio, who was French, and Palaeologus, a Greek, all the names in the earliest chapter of Unitarian history are Italian, and even these four spent greater or lesser parts of their lives in Italy. A brief listing of some of the names illustrates the background of interest and experience these Italians brought to their religious explorations: Bernardino Ochino, from Siena, at first a Catholic friar and a notable preacher; Camillo Renato, a teacher from Sicily; Francesco Negri, first an Augustinian monk, then a teacher of Hebrew; Matteo Gribaldi, professor of law at the university of Padua; Giorgio Biandrata, a physician from Piedmont; Gianpaolo Alciati, also from Piedmont, a nobleman who followed for some years a military career; Giovanni Gentile, a teacher of Latin from Naples (subsequently executed in Protestant Berne for heresy); Lelio Sozzini from Siena, who turned to theology from the family tradition of law; and the most famous of them all, his nephew Fausto Sozzini, better known by his Latinized name Faustus Socinus, and so indelibly associated with the beginnings of Unitarianism that throughout Europe the movement was for the better part of two centuries commonly called "Socinian" after him.

The re-establishment of the Italian Inquisition in 1542 marked the end of Renaissance tolerance and made Italy an uncomfortable place for independent thinkers in religion. The distinguished figures listed above all spent the latter part of their lives in exile. Only Biandrata and Socinus lived to enjoy the fellowship of organized Unitarian congregations. The others all had to work in relative isolation, communicating with each other through informal groups where this was possible and by the written word where it was not. Together they constitute a galaxy of no mean brilliance at the beginning of the story of organized

Unitarianism, and the spirit they represented spread rapidly from Italy to many other parts of Europe.

The result of this Italian influence was that from the outset Unitarianism was strongly affected by the Renaissance approach to life. Though Christianity as a whole was modified by the spirit of the new age, this came about far more slowly and reluctantly. Christian orthodoxy entered only into an uneasy dialogue with the new humanism (Protestants rejected it altogether as a part of the decadent Papal order) and for many years refused any dialogue at all with the emerging sciences. Unitarians eagerly responded to both, and contributed to the development of both.

The chief features of Renaissance humanism which had their effect upon Unitarianism were firstly, its emphasis upon things human as against the non-human, and secondly, the encouragement it gave to thinking outside the traditional patterns. Both of these became permanent features of the characteristically Unitarian point of view, held in tension within Unitarian thinking with the inherited influences of Christianity. The humanism of the Renaissance was far more concerned with human well-being and enjoyment of this life than with salvation beyond this life in the traditional Christian sense. It broadened the horizons of those it touched by introducing them to ideas and interpretations of life that found no place within the traditional scheme.

The philosophy of Greece and the religious ideas of classical antiquity had something of the broadening impact that the discovery of the great religions of eastern Asia was later to have. But Greek philosophy had its limitations too. It was almost exclusively an affair of the head rather than of the heart. The ideal Renaissance figure was first and foremost an intellectual, a rationalist, though expected also to be knowledgeable in the arts and proficient in a wide range of human activities and interests.

Moreover, this very focus upon the human promoted attitudes toward nature that were later to become disastrous in their effects both upon the human psyche and upon the world at large. The Indian sage Rabindranath Tagore pointed out the symbolism implicit in the fact that our Western thinking began within the walled cities of Greece.[1]

---

[1] Rabindranath Tagore, *Sadhana* (New York, 1913), 3.

The Spirit of the Age

Renaissance thinking too originated within walled cities, and fostered the arrogance which set human interests against those of the rest of creation, regarding the world as there for human exploitation. It was not until the walls were broken down in more recent times that this lopsided emphasis gave place to a more humble awareness of the interdependence of human life with the natural order.

Another feature of the Renaissance spirit which had a continuing influence upon Unitarian attitudes was also characteristic of the Protestant Reformation which followed the Renaissance. The prefix *Re-* in the name of both movements indicates a reference back to the past, in the one case to the classical past, in the other to early Christianity. Both made their appeal to insights of the ancient world, yet both regarded themselves as essentially progressive in their approach to the contemporary world.

Unitarians experienced the same tension between the appeal of restoring the past and that of pioneering the future. *Christianismi Restitutio* (*The Restoration of Christianity*) was the title of the book that caused the sixteenth-century Unitarian pioneer Michael Servetus to be burned at the stake. Joseph Priestley saw himself as sweeping away what he called the "corruptions of Christianity" so as to recapture its original spirit and power. "Christianity As Christ Preached It" was the title of a famous nineteenth-century Unitarian sermon that went through many printings.[2] In more recent times, the Unitarian interest in recovering ancient insights has gone far beyond the specifically Christian tradition. Yet at the same time there has always been a feeling that Unitarians belong to "the vanguard of the age," and that they are more concerned with the new that is to be brought into being than with a recovery of the old. Here again is one of the creative tensions giving rise to the dance.

The direction taken by the evolving Unitarian movement after its birth as a child of the Renaissance spirit can be understood only in terms of the major dialogue into which it entered with another child of that same spirit: the scientific revolution, which more than any other factor has moulded the modern era. Coleridge once ventured to give the credit for being the "author" of Unitarianism, in the form it took in the

---

[2] Brooke Herford, "Christianity As Christ Preached It" (c. 1853).

English-speaking world, to a man who combined the roles of scientist and religious thinker, Joseph Priestley.[3] That distinction, however, if it can realistically be accorded to any one person, must go to Priestley's far more distinguished scientific predecessor and mentor, Sir Isaac Newton.

True, Newton founded no churches. Nor did his theological writings, although they clearly set forth his Unitarianism, have any direct influence upon the movement's subsequent history. It was the incomparable impact of his scientific genius that laid the foundations for the religion of eighteenth-century Unitarians by setting forth a picture of the universe and the laws governing its operations that overturned ancient cosmologies. The words of a poet of the time capture their outlook exactly:

> Here, God-like Newton's all-capacious Mind,
> The Glory, and the Guide of Humankind,
> Shows wedded Worlds far distant Worlds embrace
> With mutual Bands, yet keep their destin'd Space ...
> Mysterious Energy! stupendous Theme!
> Immediate mover of this boundless Frame!
> Who can thy Essence, or thy Pow'r explain?
> The Sons of Wisdom seek thy Source in vain:
> Thy self invisible, yet seen thy Laws,
> This glorious Fabrick thy Effect, and God the Cause.[4]

This unitary picture of the cosmos as a mechanical system operating according to "laws that never shall be broken"[5] had the advantage of complete rationality. It was rational not because it was established by speculative argument, but because it was seen to arise out of direct observation of the way things are. "Tell me your experiments," wrote Newton. "If not, your opinion is precarious. Reasoning without experience is very slippery."[6]

---

[3] S. T. Coleridge, Table Talk, June 23, 1834.

[4] Henry Jones, *Philosophy, a Poem* (1746).

[5] "Praise the Lord! for he hath spoken; / Worlds his mighty voice obeyed; / Laws, that never shall be broken, / For their guidance he hath made." John Kempthorne, paraphrase of Psalm 148 (1810).

[6] Quoted by Carolyn Merchant, *The Death of Nature* (New York, 1980), 284.

Following Newton, the Unitarians saw God as the creator and lawgiver. The multiple conception of God expressed in the historic dogma of the Trinity had been simplified into one power sustaining the universe and operating through natural law. The existence of miracles was still accepted by Unitarians of this period, but only on the evidence of direct observation as recorded in the scriptures, a form of evidence that was not questioned until the rise of biblical criticism at a later date. In simplifying their view of the nature of the Deity to unitary form, the Unitarians had to choose between the traditional concept of the Father and that of the Holy Spirit, since the Son was obviously ineligible for the role they had in mind. It was natural that they should choose the Father, the transcendent lawgiver, and "the Fatherhood of God" became for centuries a Unitarian affirmation. In the back of their consciousness was the picture of the divine Lawgiver encountered by Moses on Mount Sinai, but delivering natural as well as moral laws.

When scientists of this period used words like "law" or "mechanism" they had no awareness at all of speaking metaphorically. These terms were used quite literally as though they gave an exact reading of the nature of things rather than an interpretation which in the final analysis was no less mythological than the ancient schemes of explanation. A twentieth-century scientist, Werner Heisenberg, can say that "what we observe is not nature in itself, but nature exposed to our method of questioning,"[7] but his eighteenth-century predecessors did not doubt that what their questioning had given them was a precise and objective picture of how the natural order worked.

This conviction was reinforced by the indisputable fact that the Newtonian theories were immensely fruitful at a practical level. They worked. Technology advanced by leaps and bounds, and was seen as opening up an immeasurably rich future for humanity. As is so often the case with new discoveries, the unfortunate side effects took some time to become apparent. But they were severe. A theology based upon a picture of God as the Holy Spirit, immanent in nature and in humanity as a part of nature, might have made it possible to avoid the mistakes that were made, but such a picture could not be reconciled with that

---

[7] W. Heisenberg, *Physics and Philosophy* (New York, 1962), 58.

of the "celestial clockmaker" standing back away from his creation and giving dominion over it to the human race. The discovery of "natural laws" was seen as a form of divine revelation intended to facilitate the exploitation of what came to be thought of as "natural resources."

The outcome of such exploitation was not only the ruination of whole ecological systems, but also a fragmentation and alienation at the human end of things. Nature was placed in opposition to culture, and it was felt that nature should be subservient to culture. Corresponding to this was an opposition within human nature itself between reason and passion, with the consequent view that passion should be subjected to reason.

Such views were by no means confined to the Unitarians of that period. They were characteristic of the leading thinkers of the day. "It was," wrote Alfred North Whitehead, "the age of reason, healthy, manly, upstanding reason; but, of one-eyed reason, deficient in its vision of depth."[8] The idea of reason, which had earlier included intuition and imagination, now became narrowed until it was synonymous with scientific method. Analysis was to break nature down into fragments that could be systematically studied in isolation, and induction would then produce from them the generalizations that constituted natural law. That much was common to all who accepted Newton as their mentor. The Deists of the period were single-minded in following this line of thought to its logical conclusion, using it to demolish and deride the entire Christian scheme of things. The Unitarians were saved from going this far by the fact that they were simultaneously involved also in the ongoing dialogue with the religious tradition, which led them to make the attempt to restate the Christian myth in terms of the scientific world-view as set forth by Newton.

The name given by historians to this phase in the evolution of modern Western thinking is the Enlightenment. In recent times it has become fashionable to pour scorn upon its unbounded faith in the possibilities of applying objective reasoning to the betterment of the human condition. Yet for all its lopsidedness – left-brained as against right-brained, it would be termed nowadays – its positive contribution was substantial as

---

[8] A. N. Whitehead, *Science and the Modern World* (Cambridge, 1932), 74.

it spread outward from the initial impetus given by the two Unitarian friends Locke and Newton in England and moved through France and Germany, eventually to cross the Atlantic and became a major influence upon the founders of the United States of America. Albert Schweitzer, indeed, looked back upon this as an age when ethical religion was an unparalleled force in the spiritual life of the time. "Ethical religion and thinking formed one unity. Thinking was religious, and religion was a thinking religion."[9] Whitehead added: "The common sense of the eighteenth century, its grasp of the obvious facts of human suffering, and of the obvious demands of human nature, acted on the world like a bath of moral cleansing... But if men cannot live on bread alone, still less can they do so on disinfectants."[10]

Locke had pioneered the way in applying Newtonian procedures to such human concerns as morals and politics. The Unitarians followed him in thinking of religion as consisting of critical thinking about ultimate matters, plus learning and following the moral laws that were to be demonstrated by similar critical processes. They shared an optimism with regard to the capacity of human beings to act as well as to think reasonably. This in turn led them to work for social reform, the aim of which was to transform existing societies according to rational ideals. Both the American and French revolutions were seen as steps in this direction, and Unitarians generally gave them their wholehearted support. Their campaigns for the abolition of slavery expressed their demand for an extension of all dimensions of freedom. "Civil and religious liberty the world over" became the watchword. Close ties were established between Unitarians and all who worked for social change, and this rapidly became another of the important dialogues shaping the evolution of the movement.

Joseph Priestley, as the "author" and embodiment of the Unitarian spirit of his day, played an outstanding role in the movements for social and political reform as well as in science and religion. It was his political radicalism, expressed boldly in times of growing reaction and repression, that led to the loss of his home and nearly of his life in the

---

[9] Charles R. Joy (ed.), *Albert Schweitzer: An Anthology* (Boston, 1947), 214.

[10] Whitehead, *Science and the Modern World*, 74.

Birmingham riots of 1791, and eventually drove him as a refugee to the United States. His ability to participate simultaneously in three of the most significant dialogues that have shaped the Unitarian movement make him a memorable figure. As one historian says of him: "He was not just the leader of a small religious minority; he was at the centre of the world's stage."[11]

But Priestley had his limitations too, and as the mood of the times changed, attention began to focus upon them. It was the poets who more than anyone pointed the finger to the lopsided sterility of a purely rationalistic approach to life, even when combined with moral fervour. William Blake denounced Locke, Newton and Priestley alike. According to Wordsworth, "the cold and rational notions of a Unitarian" expressed a form of religion that "allows no room for imagination, and satisfies none of the cravings of the soul."[12] The rise of Romanticism had begun.

It was illustrated very vividly in the career of Samuel Taylor Coleridge. As a young man Coleridge had become a Unitarian and a great admirer of Priestley, whose suffering and exile he deplored in some of his early poems. Coleridge shared in the zeal for social reform, at one time even seeing himself as a leader in establishing a Utopian community. He seriously planned to enter the Unitarian ministry. After the disenchantment that came when he began to see Unitarianism in the same light as his friend Wordsworth, he grew more and more vehement in his denunciations of the movement to which he had once belonged, ending up with the assertion that "Unitarianism is, in effect, the worst of one kind of Atheism, joined to the worst of one kind of Calvinism, like two asses tied tail to tail."[13] By this he meant, presumably, that it was an affair of the head rather than of the heart, and that its picture of God was different from his own.

Paradoxically enough, by the time this accusation was made, Unitarians themselves had begun what was to be another significant dialogue shaping their movement, and were no longer the ultra-rationalists

---

[11] H. L. Shorr, *Dissent and the Community* (London, 1962), 21.

[12] Edith J. Morley (ed.), *Henry Crabb Robinson on Books and their Writers* (London, 1938), 87.

[13] Coleridge, *Table Talk*, April 4, 1832.

The Spirit of the Age

Coleridge depicted them as being. One study of the process notes that "the curve of Coleridge's thought ... is precisely the curve more tardily followed by Unitarianism in general."[14] This may be overstating the situation, but certainly the movement as a whole broke out of the narrow scope assigned to reason in the eighteenth century and began to see it again in much broader terms, which allowed scope for intuition and imagination. The wholeness of human life was seen as including feeling and emotion no less than intellect, and the arts began to make a contribution to Unitarian life in a way not hitherto seen. For instance, whereas none of the earlier composers had been Unitarians, persons of the stature of Grieg and Bartok could so identify themselves in more recent times. This dialogue has continued productively, adding song and story, myth and symbol to the developing Unitarian tradition. The old literal and analytical approach has by no means disappeared from the contemporary Unitarian scene, and still has its place in theological debate, but it no longer plays a central role in the religion of most Unitarians, who are more interested in myth and story, art and poetry as avenues to religious insight and expressions of what is encountered in first-hand experience.

The other aspects of the early Unitarian dialogue with the spirit of the age have also continued as major influences in the movement's evolution. The social idealism which led the Polish Unitarians of the sixteenth century to espouse such daring ideas as non-violence, passive resistance and economic equality, and which flowered anew as English Unitarianism emerged as a cohesive force in the eighteenth century, continued to be a powerful force as the movement spread to other parts of the world. There was a consistent effort to establish civil and religious liberty for all, in an atmosphere of tolerance for dissenting opinions in religion, politics, economics and other fields of human concern.

Each century and each country has produced its own distinctive literature from Unitarians in support of this cause, and the authors have worked actively to remove social and legal discrimination against Jews, Catholics, women, ethnic minorities and, of course, against Unitarians themselves.

---

[14] H. N. Fairchild, *Religious Trends in English Poetry* (New York, 1949), 3:227.

The Unitarian Way

Among the Unitarians spearheading the campaign in England for the abolition of the slave trade was a member of parliament whose Liverpool constituency profited heavily from the trade. The backlash cost him his seat. In the United States many leading abolitionists were Unitarians. Equal rights for women, including the right to vote, was a cause for which Unitarians began to campaign before the end of the eighteenth century. In Britain and the United States, in Canada and Australia, successful campaigns to extend the franchise to women numbered Unitarians of both sexes among their foremost leaders.

One natural outcome of the Unitarian emphasis upon thinking for oneself has been a long-continued involvement in establishing and maintaining systems of popular and liberal education. In the days before public systems existed, Unitarian educational institutions were founded. Back in the sixteenth century, thriving universities were run under Unitarian auspices at Raków in Poland and Kolozsvár in Transylvania. At a later date came institutions of higher learning in the English-speaking world, with their curriculum slanted heavily towards the new fields of science and philosophy rather than the traditional studies of theology and the classics. Many of the existing colleges and universities both in England and America were brought into being and substantially endowed by Unitarians. Schools were also established for elementary education, while the campaign was pushed for a free public system open to everyone and devoid of all forms of sectarian indoctrination.

Other major areas of concern for Unitarians have been public health measures, the protection of those who have suffered because of their inability to defend themselves in an unregulated economic system, the extension of facilities for mental health, and penal reform. In all these fields the record of recent efforts to study the problems and promote a more enlightened attempt to tackle them is studded with the names of Unitarians. In legislative bodies, from the local to the national, Unitarians have been represented out of all proportion to their numbers, sometimes rising to the highest levels of influence (for instance, no fewer than five presidents of the United States have been Unitarians).

This devotion to activities for change and reform has earned Unitarians the reputation of being radicals not only in religion but also in politics. In each generation the current epithets of abuse reserved for those who constituted a threat to entrenched injustices have been thrown at them. The violent reaction which brought suffering and often sudden death to Unitarians of earlier generations has not been unknown in more recent times. Norbert Čapek, the leader of the Czech Unitarians, was murdered in a Nazi concentration camp; James Reeb, an American Unitarian minister, was battered to death in Selma, Alabama, during the civil rights struggles of the 1960s.

The historic Unitarian concern for building peace and international understanding has come to the fore with renewed vigour in recent years. This has been true for other religious bodies as well, and has provided a fertile field for cooperation. The observance of United Nations Day was first conceived and worked for by Unitarians in the United States.

A philosophical stance resulting from an acceptance both of social change and of the idea of a divinely-ordained natural law was the Unitarian belief in progress that reached its high-water mark late in the nineteenth century. "The progress of mankind onward and upward forever"[15] was the slogan emblazoned upon church walls as well as printed publications of that period. Progress is not simply change. It is change that is seen to conform more and more closely to ethical standards one is prepared to endorse. For a while, some Unitarians allowed themselves to be persuaded that there was something almost automatic in such a process, until the massive tragedies of the twentieth century forced a re-evaluation here as in so much religious thinking.

An additional factor in that re-evaluation, not so readily recognized, has been the change in the scientific thinking with which dialogue has to be maintained. The concept of inexorable natural law has given place to the principle of indeterminacy, which underlines the openness of a process to change in a variety of directions, and the need for ethically informed effort to move social processes in an acceptable direction. The fact that the social sciences have generally lagged behind the natural sciences in moving away from the older point of view has not helped this readjustment, but it has none the less established itself in Unitarian thinking. Optimism with regard to human progress is by no means ruled out, but such progress is now seen as coming only through

---

[15] James Freeman Clarke, "The Five Points of the New Theology" (1885).

sustained effort, with no advance assurance that the ground gained can be extended or even retained.

Important as the dialogue with the emerging sciences of the seventeenth and eighteenth centuries was for the development of Unitarian thinking, the continuation of the dialogue with science in more recent times has been equally productive. During the earlier part of this period, science seemed to be building cumulatively upon foundations already firmly laid, and bringing more and more fields of knowledge within the compass of one unified world-view. The medieval picture of the nature of things which had been so drastically revised by Newton and his successors in astronomy, physics and chemistry, was now to undergo further violent changes as a result of developments in geology and biology. These were resisted by the representatives of the status quo in religion as strenuously as the ideas of Copernicus and Galileo had been; Unitarians, however, were actively involved in the scientific researches themselves as well as in incorporating their results into their religious outlook.

The foremost Unitarian minister and theologian of nineteenth-century England, James Martineau, ministered to a congregation in London which numbered among its many distinguished members Sir Charles Lyell. More than anyone else, Lyell was responsible for demonstrating the immense age of the earth and for establishing the working principles of geology. His more famous friend, Charles Darwin, who applied his theories to biology with such earth-shattering results, was a frequent attender at the services of the same congregation. Unlike Lyell, he never became a formal member, but his Unitarian connections went back to his childhood, and he can certainly be counted among the influential contributors to the ongoing dialogue.

The general reaction from organized religion to Darwin's theories was hostile, and to this day there is a substantial and vocal segment of Christendom which entirely repudiates the concept of evolution. The traditional myths of Christianity have been interpreted very literally, as though they gave a quasi-scientific explanation of the origin of things, and the result has been the clash often dramatized as a warfare between science and theology.

Organized religion is still suffering the consequences of this clash. So too, at a deeper level, are multitudes of people who have sought in vain for a spiritual basis for living in an increasingly complex and bewildering world. To treat the imaginative myths of the religious tradition as though they were in effect scientific hypotheses was bound to discredit them. They arose in a pre-scientific era, and were never designed to conform to the canons of scientific method. In primitive life, one story might be told at one time to account for certain facts of experience, and another quite different story might be told at another time. Even at a later stage in social evolution, when the stories were written down and brought together as parts of one all-embracing mythology, variety was not sacrificed to consistency. For instance, in the earliest chapters of the Book of Genesis there are two quite distinct stories of the creation of the human race. In one of them, God creates first the animals, then human beings. In the other, the order is reversed, and Adam gives the animals their names as God creates them. Few readers seem to be bothered by this inconsistency. In fact, most of those who claim to read the Bible faithfully have probably never even noticed it.

But once the attempt is made to use scientific procedures in religion, a myth either has to be treated frankly as a product of poetic imagination or else as a literal chronicle of facts giving a scientific explanation. At first the attempt was made to choose the second alternative, with disastrous results. The great stories of the myth were transformed by the exercise of considerable ingenuity into propositions of theology which at least sounded like propositions of science:

> Man was made,
> On March the ninth, at ten o'clock in the morning
> (A Tuesday) just six thousand years ago:
> A legend of a somewhat different cast
> From the deep music of the first great phrase
> In Genesis.[16]

By contrast, the Unitarians of the late nineteenth century used evolutionary theory in the same way as their predecessors of a century earlier had used Newtonian theory. It became one of the bases of the

---

[16] Alfred Noyes, *The Torchbearers* (London, 1937), 268.

world-view underlying their religion. But they then found themselves engaged in a far less congenial dialogue with the new, inexact and controversial science of psychology. Here they found themselves threatened in much the same way as the traditionalists had been threatened by developments in the natural sciences. Freud and others began to expose the power over human life of the non-rational aspects of the personality, and thereby to undermine the Unitarian faith in human rationality.

The painful readjustment arising out of this particular dialogue has been beneficial in the long run, bringing as it does an emphasis upon the wholeness of human nature rather than upon selective aspects of it, and tempering the earlier over-optimistic reaction against the historic Christian doctrine of original sin. In the most recent period, Unitarian thinking has drawn heavily upon developing psychological theory.

The newest scientific dialogue broadens this emphasis upon wholeness to deal not simply with human nature but with the whole scheme of things. Ecology deals with relationships between the individual being and its total environment, the ecosystem. It thereby tempers another of the traditional Unitarian emphases: the focus upon individuality that can so easily degenerate into individualism. Ecological insights, on the contrary, demonstrate the intricate interdependence of all life, and this stress upon an underlying unity is certainly in accord with the spirit expressed historically in the word "Unitarian." A reaffirmation of that spirit in terms provided by recent ecological studies is one of the most productive aspects of current Unitarian thinking. It converges with the drive toward community arising out of the social concerns of the present day.

No developments in the sciences have been more far-reaching in their implications for religion than the revolutionary changes that have taken place in the theoretical basis of physics. The picture of the nature of things inherited from Newton and his predecessors presented a mechanistic model operating according to inexorable laws (with the Lawgiver standing in the background, at least until Laplace came up with his celebrated remark that he had no need of that hypothesis). By contrast, the emergence of quantum and relativity theories has produced a new model portraying an organic universe of forces and processes, consisting of patterns of energy rather than of solid substances. The traditional "laws" now become systems of interpretation supplied by the human mind. They are maps drawn to help us find our way rather than objective descriptions of a reality altogether independent of ourselves.

This new world-view is much more congenial to the essential spirit of religion than was the old mechanistic model. The parallels between the hypotheses of theoretical physics and the ancient insights of mystical religion, particularly as expressed in Eastern religions, have been repeatedly explored in the past few decades, a process that has brought a ready response from Unitarians. This might appear like a complete change of heart, in view of the substantial contribution made by Unitarians to the earlier scientific theories, but it should be noted that both Newton and Locke expressed doubts and reservations about using the mechanistic model as an all-embracing picture of the universe. It was their more single-minded disciples who ignored these qualifications and set the tone for the Age of Reason. Priestley called himself a materialist, but this could easily be misunderstood unless it is also realized that his view of the nature of matter was one which in many ways anticipated recent theories. For him, matter consisted essentially of points of force. As Channing said in his defence, he changed matter "from a substance into a power."[17]

Recent restatements of Unitarian thinking in terms of process theology and mystical holism are not so much a revolutionary change in Unitarian thinking as a re-emphasis upon elements that have always been there, but have often been overshadowed by the elements of humanism, rationalism and individualism that have also been part of the tradition.

In an era of rapid change, it is imperative to be open to new ideas. But the dialogues both with the religious traditions and with the forces shaping the life of society that have been so important an influence upon the way the Unitarian movement has developed over the past four centuries will certainly continue.

---

[17] Quoted by Alexander Gordon, *Heads of English Unitarian History* (London, 1895), 114.

10

What Do Unitarians Believe?

I was once in casual conversation with a stranger. He asked what field of work I was in. I told him that I was a minister. His reaction was immediate. "Well," he said, half-defensively, half-aggressively, "I'm afraid I'm an unbeliever!"

He didn't sound as though he was really afraid about it. It sounded more as if this was a statement in which he took considerable satisfaction. I couldn't help responding that we are all, in some senses, unbelievers. On the subject of birth control, for instance, the Pope is an unbeliever. But what fascinated me was the obvious chain of thinking out of which his statement came: I was a minister; ministers are involved with religion; religion is a matter of what you believe; there are some things that, religiously speaking, you are expected to believe; he didn't believe them; therefore he was an unbeliever.

The reason for my fascination was not that this was a strange and unheard-of line of thinking, but rather that it illustrated so simply and clearly the conventional point of view. People who are known to have a religious commitment are called "believers." The stock question to be asked about a religious community with which one is not familiar is, "What do you people believe?" By contrast, those who reject familiar forms of organized religion are called "unbelievers."

It is virtually impossible to shake some people out of this line of thinking. In vain may a Unitarian argue that religious community can be built on a basis quite different from that of shared beliefs, just as is possible in other types of community, like a family, or the crew of a ship, or a geological survey team. Still, at the end of this explanation, the question recurs: "Yes, but surely you must have *some* beliefs!" And one has to concede that of course this is true. Everyone has beliefs. They are not unimportant. Unitarians regard them as so important that each individual reserves the right to frame his or her own.

But even to say this much uses a terminology that can be misleading. The question needs to be pushed one stage further back. What, exactly, is a belief? It does not follow from the fact that this is a word that can be bandied around in argument that it stands for something that has an independent existence in its own right. In the times when many theological schemes still in existence were formulated, it was commonly thought that words are things, and that point of view survived a long time. The seventeenth-century poet Abraham Cowley hailed Francis Bacon as the deliverer from such superstitions:

> From words, which are but pictures of the thought,
> (Though we our thoughts from them perversely drew)
> To things, the mind's right object, he it brought.[1]

Such deliverance notwithstanding, nearly two centuries later, Byron could write:

> I do believe
> Though I have found them not, that there may be
> Words which are things ...[2]

Where Byron was unusual was not in believing this, but in candidly admitting that he hadn't found any. Most people seem to think they have found a great many words that are things, and the word "belief" is one of them. A belief is a thing, just as a bead is a thing – and like beads, beliefs can be strung together to form something else with an independent existence as a thing: a necklace or a creed. This can then become an heirloom, to be passed down from one generation to another.

Like Byron, I have not found any words that are things. Unlike him, I don't expect to find any. I cannot believe that there is such a thing as a belief, any more than I can believe that there is such a thing as a breath, a jump, or a pain. People breathe, people jump, they know from first-hand experience what it means to feel pain. But the breath

---

[1] Abraham Cowley, "To the Royal Society" (1668).
[2] Byron, *Childe Harold's Pilgrimage* 3.114.

and the jump and the pain are not separate things in their own right. They are simply a shorthand way of reporting how people behave or what they feel.

In the same way, a belief is simply a report on someone's behaviour. What kind of behaviour? It is as though one were feeling one's way in life, determining that one's experience and learning add up in certain ways, that certain responses to one's environment seem to be in order. It may be conceded that another person may feel it more appropriate to respond in a quite different way, and that there is no objective measurement of who is "right" or "wrong." If a number of people respond to the world in ways that are fundamentally similar, then we conventionally say that they hold the same beliefs, though this is not at all the same kind of statement as saying that they are wearing the same ties or necklaces.

It is better to stick with the verb. "What do you believe?" is a less misleading question than "What are your beliefs?" It indicates more clearly that we are talking about a living process. To be alive is to change and grow. For each one of us, our response to life requires at any given time that in certain areas our believing is strong enough for us to stake our lives upon it. There are other areas in which our believing may be strong enough for us to say we have reasonable assurance. There are others again in which believing and doubting co-exist within us in an unresolved struggle, and yet others where we may "try on a belief for size" almost playfully, to see what validity it might have. Conventionally, we make "things" of all these processes, and say we have convictions, beliefs, opinions, hypotheses, doubts and reservations. Each day will bring some modification in the way this combination is arranged within the life of each of us, as we respond to new experiences, ideas and persons.

So it is proper to ask not only, "Do you believe that?," but "How strongly do you believe that?" Sometimes, indeed, a person's inner condition may be such that no answer is possible to either question. You may, on the one hand, hover between the equally strong considerations that seem to exist on both sides of the issue, or else the issue itself may seem so inconsequential in terms of your real concerns that it has never seemed necessary to establish any opinion about it. As an instance of the first kind of situation, many people may find it difficult to make up their minds whether they feel that abortion is right or wrong. But a

What Do Unitarians Believe?

woman with an unwanted pregnancy is forced into coming to a conclusion one way or the other within a limited space of time. Life often forces decision-making in this way, which brings out into the light of day what you believe, however strongly or weakly you believe it. The same situation confronts a conscientious objector to war faced with military conscription. This is, as we say, the moment of truth. Then you find out what you really believe, however much you may have evaded making up your mind until that moment.

But there are other matters on which, for many of us, there is no moment of truth, no compulsion to believe one way or the other. Years ago, someone asked me whether Unitarians believe in the Immaculate Conception. I had to reply that this was so far outside what Unitarians even think about that I doubted whether many of them had ever felt it necessary to ask themselves whether they believed it or not. We reserve belief or disbelief for matters that are important to us.

But at any given time, there are matters concerning which we may frame a statement of personal belief. The process of articulating such a statement is very much like that of having a photograph taken. The photograph shows us as we were and where we were at a specific time. By the time it can be printed and shown to other people it is already slightly out of date. As time goes by, it becomes more radically out of date. One cannot apply for a new passport with an old photograph.

The danger in giving beliefs an assumed existence of their own is that they are thereby invested with a degree of permanence that is not true to life. They can still be repeated as though they represented current thinking, just as poring over old photographs can give rise to the impression that nothing has changed since they were taken. The repetition of the words in a creed is only an extreme example of this process. The thinking that is pressed and dried in the words may in fact have been one's own at one particular stage in one's life-story. Some years ago a professional philosopher wrote this remarkable confession, as he looked back at one period in his life:

> The many words I wrote and said were not the expression of a mind engaged in thinking things out afresh, but of a mind which was living on the deposit of thought that it had laid down in the past. I was stirring and re-applying, but not adding to the old material. In fact, I was like a

rentier living on the income derived from the capital his ancestors had accumulated, for it is as his ancestor that the middle-aged man of forty is entitled to regard the young man of twenty who formed his mind.[3]

This is not to say that one should never try to set down in words what one believes about the really significant issues of life. On the contrary, the exercise of doing precisely this is often required if one is to clarify one's own thinking and test it in dialogue with others. Such dialogue may result in substantial agreement, in which case it is conventionally said that we "hold the same beliefs." And in point of fact, Unitarians do in this way hold the same beliefs on many matters. Those who do not share them would not feel at home in a Unitarian community.

It is nonsense for critics to say that one can believe whatever one likes and still be a Unitarian. It is not possible to believe in the virtues of racism, totalitarianism, irrationalism and dogmatism and still be a Unitarian. It is not possible to repudiate all concern for the well-being of one's fellows and still be a Unitarian. It is not possible to believe that life is totally worthless and meaningless and still be a Unitarian. There is a Unitarian consensus on major principles, though not on the specifics that represent the individual character of each one of us, and these common principles are capable of being articulated in words. The question "What do Unitarians believe?", though it has to be approached very cautiously, is not therefore an altogether inappropriate one.

Belief in unity – an ultimate underlying unity – is the best place to begin in looking for a Unitarian consensus, for this is one characteristic of the movement that has been noted by friends and foes alike throughout its history, and has, indeed, given it its name. Of the many points from which one could begin an examination of this theme, there is one that strikes home vividly because, although it addresses itself directly to concerns that loom large at the present day, it was in fact written back in the nineteenth century by one of the major figures in the Unitarian tradition. Ralph Waldo Emerson, in one of his poems, wrote of his disenchantment with dominant attitudes toward the world in which we live and of which we form part. Wistfully he hoped that

---

[3] C. E. M. Joad, *God and Evil* (London, 1942), 14.

> ... I could be a part
> Of the round day, related to the sun
> And planted world, and full executor
> Of their imperfect functions.

Such a hope was far removed from that of those who set the patterns for thinking about the relationship of the human to the non-human, whom he called "thieves and pirates of the universe." The dominant attitude toward our surroundings, he said, is to "invade them impiously for gain; we devastate them unreligiously."

> ... These young scholars who invade our hills,
> Bold as the engineer who fells the wood,
> And travelling often in the cut he makes,
> Love not the flower they pluck, and know it not,
> And all their botany is Latin names.

In earlier days, by contrast, there were those who showed a wiser attitude by

> Preferring things to names, for these ...
> Were unitarians of the united world,
> And wheresoever their clear eye-beams fell,
> They caught the footsteps of the SAME.[4]

Romanticized though this account of the Unitarian outlook of a bygone era may be, it none the less expresses an authentic insight into basic Unitarian attitudes. At the end of the nineteenth century another Unitarian prophet, Jabez T. Sunderland, in words reprinted many times on both sides of the Atlantic, wrote:

> Unitarianism, to be true to its great name, must be the religion of the Eternal Unities ... All the religious faiths in their deeper meanings are one; all social interests are one; humanity is one; all life is strangely one; all worlds unite to make one orderly and harmonious universe. The mission of Unitarianism is nothing less than to be faithful to this truth, in all that is deepest and most religiously significant in it.[5]

Traditionally, this Unitarian vision has found expression as a belief in the undivided unity of God. The Unitarian churches of Transylvania,

---

[4] R. W. Emerson, "Blight."

[5] J. T. Sunderland, "The Larger Meaning of Unitarianism" (1883).

which have survived more than four centuries of adversity, still prominently display their historic affirmation, *Egy az Isten*: God is one. That this statement should have evoked such depth of feeling, not only for Hungarian-speaking Unitarians but for English-speaking Unitarians as well, indicates that it symbolizes something very fundamental. One does not put up with long-continued social pressures and persecution for something that is inconsequential.

The power of the historic affirmation arises from the fact that it commits those who accept it to be "unitarians of the united world." If the world is perceived as united, then underlying all its diversities there is one essential principle of coherence. They called this "God." To be sure, that word has often been used in the plural as well as in the singular, but it has always stood for what is conceived to be most basic, most permanent and most significant in the whole scheme of things. And Unitarians perceived this as a unity that would make sense of the endless diversity we encounter as we go through this life.

One of the most honoured names in Unitarian history is that of William Ellery Channing. Back in the year 1826 he delivered a forceful summary of the Unitarian thinking of his time, declaring that

> it presents to the mind one, and only one ... distinct and intelligible object of worship ... The more strict and absolute the unity of God, the more easily and intimately all the impressions and emotions of piety flow together, and are condensed into one glowing thought, one thrilling love.
>
> ... Unitarianism is in accordance with nature. Philosophy, in proportion as it extends its views of the universe, sees in it, more and more, a sublime and beautiful unity.[6]

This first affirmation among the shared beliefs of Unitarians is reinforced by the growing ecological consciousness of the present time. We live in a universe, not a multiverse. Unitarians believe in wholeness and peace, in an ultimate unity that is fractured only at the cost of courting total destruction. This holistic approach is equally applicable whether we are talking about ultimate reality, the nature of the cosmos, the web of life on our planet, international politics, personal ethics or the structure of an individual personality. Unitarians believe in unity.

---

[6] *The Works of W. E. Channing* (Boston, 1883), 387, 392.

What Do Unitarians Believe?

The second major belief shared by Unitarians is a positive affirmation of life. At first glance, this may not seem sufficiently distinctive to rank as anything more than a general platitude, but a moment's reflection will serve to remind us that many forms of religion vigorously depreciate what they call "this life" in favour of some other realm of being to be entered upon when this life is over. We are, they tell us, pilgrims through a vale of sin and woe in which nothing has value in itself, but only as a means to help us move forward to something better that is seen as lying beyond death.

In accordance with their unitary approach, Unitarians draw no such sharp distinction between the conditions of our being in the here and now and whatever may be regarded as the goal toward which we may hope to move. All life is ultimately one, though it may be experienced in many different dimensions with a wide range of value. There are times when an individual may feel that his or her life is not worth living, and there are times when an objective observer would find it difficult to quarrel with that assessment. But whatever may be the case in an individual situation, this does not invalidate the worth of life itself. Individuals come and go. Life goes on, and to the extent that we transcend the limits of individuality and participate in the wider life that is the life of all, we are able to experience its positive values whatever our individual situation. Life itself can be affirmed even in face of deprivation and suffering, and a sense of its ultimate sacredness can spur us to resist the threat to life as a whole posed by the engines of destruction produced by human ingenuity during the past century.

To put the matter in another way, the Unitarian approach is a hopeful one, affirming that the values we cherish can indeed become a reality in this world and this life, though not without costly effort. In the palmy period before 1914 there were many Unitarians who endorsed that era's widespread belief in an almost automatic progress toward a high quality of life. No one feels tempted to accept such a facile position today, but with the violent swing of the pendulum it becomes all the more necessary not to lose hope.

Reference was made in an earlier chapter to Albert Schweitzer's prophetic utterances on the prospects of our civilization. But despite his gloomy assessment, he added significantly, "To the question whether I am a pessimist or an optimist, I answer that my knowledge is pessimistic, but my willing and hoping are optimistic."[7] Many other reflective thinkers have expressed themselves in similar terms. Though a strictly objective intellectual accounting would lead to pessimistic conclusions, such a person remains committed to the option that leads to life. Describing an address he gave to his fellow-sufferers in a Nazi concentration camp, Viktor Frankl wrote: "I told them that … I estimated my own chances at about one in twenty. But I also told them that, in spite of this, I had no intention of losing hope and giving up."[8] Twenty years earlier the brilliant Italian radical Antonio Gramsci, subsequently martyred by Mussolini, adopted as his motto "pessimism of the intellect; optimism of the will."[9] Not only does this express a stance that commends itself to Unitarians at the present time; it has a message for humanity as a whole in an era when pessimism with regard to future prospects becomes the increasingly credible attitude.

Unitarians, then, are committed to an affirmation of life in face of all life-threatening forces. But life is more than simple existence. One feature of human experience that has impressed itself indelibly upon religious thinking all down the ages is that it becomes necessary to speak in terms of quality of life. The question as to whether the quality of life can rise to levels which can transcend all the ravages of time has been one of the perennial topics of religious speculation. It is not simply a matter of what might or might not come after the death of an individual (for that death is still an event in time) but of whether there may be dimensions of life to which the passage of time is totally irrelevant. The traditional term for life liberated from bondage to time is eternal life, though in much popular usage this has come to mean an endless continuation within time. Eternal life, properly understood, stands for a condition of being in which there is no past or future, but rather a

---

[7] Albert Schweitzer, *Out of my Life and Thought* (New York, 1933), 240.

[8] Viktor Frankl, *Man's Search for Meaning* (New York, 1963), 130.

[9] This motto has generally been associated with Gramsci, who used it on the masthead of his newspaper *L'Ordine Nuovo*, and repeatedly in his other writings; however, he himself claimed it was coined by the novelist Romain Rolland.

participation in a different dimension altogether, in which the ultimate values of life come to fruition. Here lies the goal of our seeking when we speak of a positive affirmation of life.

Closely allied to this affirmation of life is a hopeful belief in the potentialities of human nature. This can be contrasted with the outlook of those forms of religion that lay heavy stress upon the depths of depravity to which human nature can sink – an outlook illustrated classically in the words of the Westminster Confession: "we are utterly indisposed, disabled and made opposite to all good, and wholly inclined to all evil." No very exacting survey of the current world scene is called for to verify the plausibility of such a pessimistic view. It seems to be validated by a glance at the headlines in any newspaper, and it requires more of an effort of thought to remind oneself that dramatic examples of evil behaviour are precisely the stuff of which headlines are made. Decent behaviour seems less spectacular, and is less often reported. Can it be that this is because we instinctively expect such behaviour, and therefore feel it unnecessary to call attention to it? We would hardly do that if we believed wholeheartedly in human depravity.

But more than decent behaviour exists, even if often unreported. One has to ask why human nature should be judged in terms of its expression in Genghis Khan rather than Jesus Christ, in Adolf Hitler rather than Albert Einstein. Depending upon how one selects the facts that are to be regarded as admissible evidence, it is possible to make a case for human nature as either saintly or devilish. It is unfortunate that once this has been recognized, the natural tendency seems to be to proceed, consciously or unconsciously, to the assumption that my friends and I are the saints and that those we regard as our enemies are the devils. This application of a lopsided theology can be particularly disastrous in the international arena.

A more realistic understanding of the situation accepts that the polarity between what we call good and what we call evil runs not simply through the human race but through each one of us as an individual, and further, that like all other polarities, this one is capable of being transcended within a greater whole.

The Unitarian Way

Human nature, however varied the forms of expression it may take in different individuals and within the same individual, is neither a constant nor an isolated phenomenon. It is not constant because it is continually changing and growing, and reflects the level in the evolutionary process that has thus far been reached. It is not isolated because human beings do not live in isolation. We are what we are as a result of continuous interaction with an environment that is not separated from our own essential nature by any impenetrable boundary. We are all of us continually being defined and redefined by the whole constellation of relationships into which we enter.

The living of my life, in a physical sense, is a continuous process of incorporating new molecules into the ever-changing pattern which constitutes my identity. The new molecules replace others which are continually being lost, so that elements that were once part of my body (or rather, of me in a physical sense, for my body is not a detachable possession in the way my house is) are now part of new organized systems of many kinds in many parts of the world.

In precisely the same way, the living of my life in what may be called a spiritual sense is a continuous process of incorporating new relationships into the ever-changing pattern which constitutes my identity. Just as in a physical sense the quality of living is enhanced, first by the incorporation into my body of those beneficial elements which make for the best possible functioning of the whole, and then by an adequate exercising of the whole, so too in a spiritual sense the quality of living is enhanced by multiplication and exercise of my positive relationships to the cosmos as a whole, to the world of living things, and to other human beings. If this process ceases in either the physical or the spiritual dimension, then I am no longer really alive.

"The individual is a fact of existence insofar as he steps into a living relation with other individuals," wrote Martin Buber.[10] Such a living relationship obviously means something a great deal closer and more positive than simply being in the neighbourhood of others. It requires not simply an understanding of the definition of being a neighbour, but also the active response of loving one's neighbour as oneself. This point is well illustrated by the way in which Jesus responded when asked by

---

[10] Martin Buber, *Between Man and Man* (Boston, 1955), 203.

a lawyer for a definition of what he meant by "neighbour." He told the story of the Samaritan who rescued the man beaten up by brigands. The relationship came alive.

Human nature as it finds expression in any one individual can be assessed in terms of the number of such significant relationships that intersect within that individual. That number is always changing, and can change in either direction. So asking whether human nature is good or evil is like asking whether water is hot or cold. The real question is not asked in the abstract, but demands a direct look at the number of relationships with the human and the non-human neighbourhood that intersect within this particular person.

One further aspect of such relationships is important. There are experiments in chemistry where under certain conditions one crystal may be dropped into a solution and precipitates the immediate formation of a great many more crystals like itself. In the same way, one person who stands at the point of intersection where many positive relationships meet may induce their intersection at other points as well, and thus strengthen the living and loving of others. It is this possibility that holds out hope for human society as well as for the human individual, in days when such hope comes far from easily.

This view of human nature and conduct demands a fresh and creative response to each new person and each new situation. It therefore stands at the other end of the spectrum from that strict observance of rules and commandments, supposed to cover all possibilities, in which the carrying out of "religious duties" has often been thought to consist. The basic objection to such commandments is that they place a straitjacket upon one's freedom to respond creatively to the uniqueness of each situation in which one finds oneself, and instead sort life out into prescribed categories within each of which there is a stereotyped response. The same objections arise as with creeds at an intellectual level. But like creeds, commandments are not totally useless. They can be regarded as maxims expressing some sort of consensus as to the best procedures in very generalized situations. Carry them further than this and they choke the individual's growth and development.

Such growth and development are always seen by Unitarians as open possibilities. Unitarians believe in the potentialities of human nature.

11

Wider Horizons

Another major Unitarian affirmation is a belief in universality, which excludes all exclusiveness. No one person, no one faith, no one book, no one institution has all the answers, nor even any patent on the way of finding answers. Inspiration, discovery, insight, wisdom: these are to be found among people belonging to all religious traditions, coming from all parts of the earth and from all periods of history. Religion as a universal feature of human life is broader than the specific forms taken by the various institutions and traditions that call themselves religions.

Unitarians believe in a universal humanity underlying all the cultural and political institutions that the various races and nations have developed. Unitarians believe that outstanding personages such as Jesus and Socrates and the Buddha are part of our common humanity, not intrusions from the outside. They attained heights that can be reached also by others within this same common humanity, and no doubt have been on many occasions.

Such an affirmation is challenged by the claims to uniqueness and exclusiveness made by many ideologies and religions. In the Western world, such claims most frequently arise out of the Christian tradition with which Unitarians have been engaged in so longstanding a dialogue. They are advanced on behalf of the unique significance of Jesus as a person and of the Bible as a literary source. The persistence of such exclusive claims has often made it appear that Unitarian inclusiveness consists more of denials than of affirmations. Unitarians, it is claimed, don't believe in Christ.

If the term Christ is to be interpreted in such a way as to give Jesus a uniquely superhuman status, then discussion of this allegation ends before it begins. But this is to ignore the way in which the term has in fact been used by many perceptive persons both inside and outside the Christian tradition. For them it points to a spiritual stature to which a human being can attain when that person transcends the limitations of individuality and becomes an active and conscious embodiment of the universal spiritual nature.

Jesus expressed such a consciousness when he declared, using the paternal metaphor that was so marked a feature of his poetic use of language, "I and the Father are one!"[1] Whether we choose to call this an expression of Christ-consciousness, or mysticism, or essential relatedness to the ultimate nature of things, what we are doing is simply selecting one vocabulary rather than another. The point is, however, that no matter which vocabulary we choose, we are not implying that there is something exclusive in such a claim. What Jesus was here experiencing may be and has been experienced by many others who have attained, in the words of Paul the Apostle, to "the measure of the stature of the fullness of Christ."[2]

The Christ-spirit is therefore a universal feature of human life, finding fuller expression in the lives of some persons than of others, but in no way confined to only one person. However, another universal feature of human psychology must also be reckoned with. As Emerson once put it, "The universal does not attract us until housed in an individual."[3] Political liberators as well as religious prophets have been seen as living incarnations of universal principles, and this has endowed them with a powerful influence over the feelings and imagination of their followers. In fact, the need for a personality of this kind is such that if no such person actually existed, there is an almost irrepressible urge to invent one. From time to time it has been argued that Jesus was an imaginary rather than historical figure. While such theories may be far-fetched in this particular instance, they are much more likely to be correct with regard to Moses or Zoroaster or Lao-tzu. If these were actual persons, they probably bore little resemblance to the legendary figures who now bear their names.

---

[1] John 10:30.

[2] Ephesians 4:13.

[3] R. W. Emerson, "Nominalist and Realist."

The veneration with which such persons are treated results in their being credited with superhuman deeds, or even with being born of the seed of the gods. Jesus, as described in an earlier chapter, became transfigured into the central figure of a mythology which has had an incalculable influence upon human history.

The danger in exclusive attachment to one religious or political hero is that it can all too easily degenerate into a cult of the individual. Whatever such a person says or does is then automatically approved. Any criticism is seen as tantamount to treason.

Some religious traditions, such as Christianity and Islam, set their focus primarily upon one personality. Even here, however, other saints and seers within the tradition are treated as lesser leaders and examples. This broadening of the focus is much more pronounced in religions such as Judaism and Hinduism, which acknowledge a whole range of spiritual guides without giving complete pre-eminence to any. Unitarianism stands at the far end of this spectrum, acknowledging spiritual attainments in whatever person they may be found, irrespective of religious tradition or period of history. It is on the basis of such a wide-ranging appreciation that most Unitarians would acknowledge the spiritual greatness of Jesus.

Who was Jesus? How far can one get beyond legends and theological creeds to discover the real person, Yeshua ben Yusuf as he would have been known in his own Aramaic language, who once walked the hills of Palestine?

A great deal is known about the world in which he lived. The Roman Empire was at the height of its power. It controlled the whole Mediterranean basin and areas far beyond. But the cultural influences in the eastern part of the Empire were still predominantly Greek, which was the international language of that area. The Jewish nation into which Yeshua was born was keenly sensitive to its oppression by foreign imperialists, and from time to time rebellions broke out. The rows of crosses upon hilltops were a familiar sight, for the Romans used this hideously cruel method of public execution as a deterrent to would-be rebels.

The whole country was seething with unrest and yearning for liberation. Rumours that the Messiah would appear as a national saviour swept around the streets and bazaars. As to the nature of the liberation

Wider Horizons

that was to come, there were differences of opinion. Some expected a military revolt, and this eventually came about, with disastrous consequences, in the years 66-70. But others were disenchanted with military or political action and were more inward-looking. They would be liberated, they felt, by meditation and spiritual exercises rather than by trying to overthrow the system.

It was into this scene that Yeshua arrived, preaching the coming of the kingdom of heaven, an ambiguous phrase that could be understood to mean either a new social order or an inward spiritual condition. As long as there was any possibility that it could be taken to mean the former, the authorities could not afford to take any chances. Such a man was dangerous. He had to be, and was, removed. Always and everywhere, ruthless power has one ultimate and supposedly final way of getting rid of trouble-makers: death. The problem is, however, that this does not always turn out to be the final solution. Even when the cause is one of political liberation, there is often the conviction that although the leader has fallen the work will go on until the battle is finally won. When the cause is one of spiritual liberation, then the forces at work are even more potent, because few if any religions are prepared to concede the finality of death. Certainly this was so in the case of Yeshua. His followers were convinced that death was not the end of him, that in a very real sense he lived on as a powerful presence in their midst. The strength of that conviction eventually transformed Yeshua ben Yusuf into Jesus Christ, who was alive for evermore.

What more can be said about the historical personage whom we call Jesus? Scholars have toiled for years to answer this question, with few positive results to show for their work. The records are sparse, hazy and at times mutually contradictory. They have been overlaid with the interpretations of later generations. No reporters accompanied Jesus with shorthand notebooks or voice recorders; the words now attributed to him were written down in Greek many years after he originally spoke in Aramaic. We read them, usually, in a further translation into English. It would be absurd to pretend that we are in possession of his exact words, which is what popular preaching often presupposes.

One of the more revealing experiments of recent years attempts to retranslate the words of the Greek texts back into what may have been the original Aramaic. When this is done, the seemingly pedestrian prose sometimes comes alive in poetic patterns, confirming the instinctive feeling many people have had that Jesus was essentially a poet. This was the characteristic language of the Hebrew prophets, captivating their hearers and making their message easy to remember.

One other feature that comes across clearly from the records, scanty though they are, is that Jesus spoke out of personal first-hand spiritual awareness. We are told that what he said struck his hearers as having the ring of authority, by contrast with what was said by the scribes. These latter were pedantic teachers of other people's ideas handed down from the past. Jesus too could quote from what had been said by others, but when he did so it was to illustrate the perennial insights that had been a part of the consciousness of others and were now in equal measure a part of his. These were universal truths that had come alive once again in an individual person.

The core of Jesus' teaching is expressed in the one summons attributed to him as to his predecessor John the Baptist: "Repent, for the kingdom of heaven is close at hand!"[4] Since this was misunderstood even in his own time, it may seem rash to venture an explanation, but one or two points do seem to be clear. First, repentance should not be confused, as it so often is, with remorse. Repentance is forward-looking, remorse backward-looking. Repentance means a reorientation of one's whole life in the light of new insights that have been gained. As for the kingdom of heaven, this seems to represent a perception of what is basic, eternal, in the nature of things, and the call of Jesus was that we should come to recognize this and align our lives with it, instead of following the disastrous course of thinking that we can find our own way in life on the basis of short-term self-centred motivations.

That message obviously has a timeless character, however seldom it may have been taken fully to heart by those who have heard it. Jesus compared those who did attempt to put it into practice with the yeast at work in three measures (i.e. 25 kilograms) of flour – a demanding process. When the yeast really is at work, it shows its results in a way of life that is not dominated by rules and regulations, but grows as naturally

---

[4] Matthew 3:2, 4:17, 10:7. See also Mark 1:15, Luke 10:9-11.

as the lilies of the field to which Jesus appealed by way of illustration. J. Estlin Carpenter, a perceptive Unitarian interpreter writing a century ago, summed it up thus:

> The morality of Jesus is inward rather than outward. This does not mean that he was indifferent to conduct. Action is one of his persistent demands: "by their fruits shall ye know them" ... His teaching does not emphasize specific acts so much as the quality of being. Much of it is not even new; its originality consists in giving fresh values to the old. It is a morality not of law but of affection.[5]

If this is really so, then it follows that the spirit of Jesus must be distorted in any attempt to make him the focus of exclusive claims. The Unitarian spirit of inclusiveness seems to be closer to what he stood for in his living and teaching. In fact, it was what he explicitly called for, if we may trust the attempts to translate back from the Greek to the Aramaic. In the Sermon on the Mount, as it is usually rendered, Jesus is represented as saying "You must be perfect, as your heavenly Father is perfect!"[6] This sounds like a tough requirement, for it is proverbial that nothing human is perfect.

But it turns out that in Aramaic the wording would have meant, "You must be all-inclusive, just as your heavenly Father is all-inclusive," which certainly makes sense of the way Jesus goes on to illustrate the all-inclusiveness of the heavenly Father by describing how he makes the sun to shine on the evil and on the good and sends rain on the just and on the unjust. Here we move with the naturalness of the seasons. Their rhythms move in our lives too, as we become loving and all-inclusive.

The same inclusive spirit must govern a Unitarian response to exclusive claims made on behalf of the Bible. A literature no less than a person speaks directly to us when we find within it universal truths that illuminate our particular personal or social condition. The Bible is a miscellaneous collection of documents, the most recent of which are nearly two thousand years old. The exact number varies according to whether the compilers were Catholic, Protestant or Jewish, but in each case the documents are presented within the covers of a single

---

[5] J. Estlin Carpenter, *The First Three Gospels* (London, 1906), 374.

[6] Matthew 5:48.

volume. Some sections are of little interest except as chronicles of folklore, political intrigue or military struggle. But no Unitarian would wish to downplay either the literary beauty or the spiritual insights to be found in parts of the Bible. Alongside these they would place other treasures to be found elsewhere in ancient or modern literature, whether or not this has been hallowed by any religious tradition as scripture in the conventional meaning of that word. A Unitarian response to any such literature is determined by whether (in Jacob Boehme's memorable metaphor) this turns out to be "the hammer that can strike my bell."[7]

We proceed now to the most universal and ultimate question of all. No examination of religious belief could even present the appearance of being complete if it did not at some point or other come to grips with the question which in recent history has usually taken the form: "Do you believe in God?"

What kind of process is believing-in-God? The popular assumption that it consists simply of thinking and speaking is one that many others besides Unitarians have questioned. Perhaps the answer to the question "Do you believe in God?" should consist in an attempt to tell the story of one's life. What kind of priorities do I establish in my living? Some persons have answered that question by painting a picture, composing music, building a cathedral.

But words are the only medium available here, however inadequate they may be and however great the probabilities of misunderstanding. The Catholic philosopher Gabriel Marcel wrote:

> The answer to a referendum on the question, "Do you believe in God?" ought to be in the great majority of cases, "I don't know whether I believe in God or not – and I am not even quite sure that I know what 'believing in God' is." Note, carefully, the contrast between these formulae and those of the agnosticism of the [nineteenth] century: "I don't know whether there is a God or not."[8]

Philosophers, like scientists, have moved a long way since the nineteenth century, but it remains true that most popular discussion

---

[7] Jacob Boehme, *The Signature of All Things* (1621), 1:1.
[8] Gabriel Marcel, *The Mystery of Being* (London, 1950), 1:12.

Wider Horizons

in both fields is still based upon that century's presuppositions. Those presuppositions took it for granted that some questions were resolved. For instance, the unifying tendency derived from Newtonian science determined that there could only be one God, at most. For the greater part of human history, stories had been told which pictured a whole pantheon of gods, and in cultures which the nineteenth century called "primitive" or even "savage," such pictures persisted. They corresponded to some directly experienced aspects of life. Does life as we experience it seem to come together into a harmony and unity, or is our most basic experience one of multiplicity and discord?

For most of us, if we are to be honest, experience points both ways. Sometimes one feeling is dominant, sometimes the other. That is why so many forms of religion have tried to combine unity with multiplicity in their pictures of what gives ultimate meaning to the universe as it is. Christianity provides not only the doctrine of the Trinity, combining unity and plurality, but also a pantheon of angels and glorified saints, each the patron of some aspect of our life-experience. In Hinduism, which stresses an ultimate all-inclusive unity more strongly perhaps than any other of the great historical religions, multiplicity breaks out all over the place in an exuberant interplay of gods and goddesses.

But nineteenth-century Western thinkers had come to a point where they felt that only one concept of God was worthy of discussion: the concept of a single God, the architect of the universe, creator and sustainer of all things, with whom human beings could maintain a person-to-person relationship. If you gave your assent to this picture, you were called a theist. If you rejected it, you were called an atheist. If you felt you could live without making up your mind one way or the other, you were called an agnostic. But all parties were agreed in accepting the Thwackum definition.

In spite of the efforts of contemporary theologians from many traditions, most discussion of belief in God still remains at that level. An arbitrary definition, usually drawn from traditional Christian theology, is taken as the starting point, and the argument is over whether any reality exists corresponding to that definition. This is precisely the procedure that was condemned centuries ago by that perceptive Catholic mystic

Meister Eckhart: "Whoever seeks God under settled form lays hold of the form, while missing the God concealed in it."[9]

The traditional term for this is idolatry. In much of the ancient Hebrew tradition, there was such a horror of idolatry that the use of the word "God" was formally forbidden. One could use all sorts of circumlocutions to allude to God indirectly, but one could not speak of God directly. The same has been true right down to the present day in strict Jewish circles. As Erich Fromm notes, "the biblical prohibition of any kind of representation of God, and against using God's name in vain, means that one can talk *to* God in prayer, in the act of relating oneself to God, but one must not talk *about* God lest God be transformed into an idol."[10]

This attempt to avoid idolatry has led in many instances to people being popularly tarred as atheists. That term was applied to Socrates and to Spinoza, both of them profoundly religious persons who were unwilling to accept the Thwackum definitions provided by their contemporaries. In the same vein, the Roman emperor Julian asked, "Are we refusing to face the fact that Atheism owes its success above all to its philanthropy towards strangers and to its provision for funerals and to its parade of a high puritanical morality?"[11] The people of whom he was speaking were the early Christians, whose "atheism" consisted in a refusal to acknowledge the gods of Rome.

Is it then impossible to speak of God at all? Many sensitive people have thought so. The modern Indian philosopher Radhakrishnan wrote: "Those who live in God do not care to define. They have a peculiar confidence in the universe, a profound and peaceful acceptance of life in all its sides ... An austere silence is more adequate to the experience of God than elaborate descriptions."[12] The Western theologian Paul Tillich was more venturesome, but still stopped far short of dogmatic definition. "The word God," he wrote, "means in all religions that which

---

[9] Meister Eckhart, as quoted by Aldous Huxley, *The Perennial Philosophy* (London, 1964), 324.

[10] Erich Fromm, *You Shall Be as Gods* (Greenwich, CT, 1966), 28.

[11] Arnold Toynbee, *An Historian's Approach to Religion* (London, 1956), 97.

[12] Carl Hermann Voss (ed.), *The Universal God* (New York, 1953), 34.

is ultimate in being and in meaning, that which is the ground and foundation of being and not *a* being alongside others."[13]

It is in the light of such utterances that the general Unitarian reluctance to bandy the word God around has to be seen. Unitarians too have been called atheists, and in view of popular conceptions of God, some have accepted that designation. But it is by one's way of life that one must ultimately be judged, not by the words one uses or does not use. It may be sufficient to have a humility and reverence toward the mystery of being, an attempt to live by the highest values, and a feeling of essential oneness with what Wordsworth called

> ... something far more deeply interfused,
> Whose dwelling is the light of setting suns.[14]

How does one express one's relationship to such a felt reality? In a way of life, certainly, but a more immediate response is indicated in Erich Fromm's description, quoted above, of the traditional Jewish attitude: "one can talk *to* God in prayer ... but one must not talk *about* God." But are words really any more indispensable in the one case than in the other? Prayer is central in religious practice, but its forms vary as widely as do pictures of God. There are those for whom it means, in effect, telephoning an order to the proprietor of a cosmic department store. There are those for whom it means grovelling and imploring before a magnified despotic ruler. There are those who believe that, as in the *Arabian Nights*, the door will not open unless the precise words of the magic formula are uttered. On the other hand, the prayer of silent meditation or contemplation has been a feature of the deeper forms of religion in all traditions, and it is this that Unitarians tend to find most meaningful. Where words are used, they are understood to be essentially poetic in character.

Do Unitarians believe in God? In their resistance to being thrust into the straitjacket that the question implies, contemporary Unitar-

---

[13] Paul Tillich, "The Idea of God as Affected by Modern Knowledge." Garvin Lecture delivered in the Unitarian Church in Lancaster, Pennsylvania, November 27, 1957.

[14] Wordsworth, "Lines Composed above Tintern Abbey."

ians echo the sentiments expressed by their predecessor Ralph Waldo Emerson: "Do not speak of God much. After a very little conversation on the highest nature, thought deserts us and we run into formalism."[15]

---

[15] R. W. Emerson, *Journals* (Cambridge, MA, 1914), 4:475.

12

Dimensions of Community

Believing is essentially an individual matter. That is why the question of allegedly "shared beliefs" has been such a thorny and divisive one in religious history. Discussions of belief do not come first in any presentation of the Unitarian way because Unitarians find the ties that unite their community at an entirely different level. What they are attempting to do is to combine individual integrity of life and thought with participation in a nurturing community that can work together cooperatively and productively.

This calls for the kind of structure and organization that will facilitate such a process. The Unitarian movement, like any other religious body that persists through any substantial period of time, has its institutional structure, the skeleton that supports the living tissues. Though such structures are maintained at all levels up to and including the international level, there has never been any doubt that the basic unit is a local one, in which the group life is such that the members have ample opportunity to know each other at a person-to-person level.

In a local congregation, each member can participate fully in the process of democratic decision-making. There is seldom complete unanimity, but there is usually a broad consensus which reflects not only the contributions of the current members but also that of those who have preceded them and established an ongoing tradition. A church has been called a community of memory and hope. Shared memories mean that it builds upon the work of the past; shared hopes mean that it works together in the present to build for the future. If (as it was put by the early nineteenth-century writer quoted earlier) Unitarians take love as their bond of union, this expresses itself in a sharing of memories and hopes, experiences and ideas, feelings and values and commitments. The objective is to frame a response to life that will do justice to its depth, breadth and rich variety. The community seeks ways of living in today's world with sensitivity and integrity.

How can it organize to pursue these ends most effectively? One way of looking at the process is to refer back to the illustration in Chapter 5 that shows the symbol of the flaming chalice dividing the circle into four quadrants. Each of these can be seen as representing a vital aspect of congregational life. Together they make up a complete community, and must be seen in this light, for each demands the others and can never be detached from them.

The four components thus comprising the whole can be expressed as, first, the church as a worshipping community; second, the church as a learning and teaching community; third, the church as a sharing and caring community; fourth, the church as a socially responsible community that reaches out into the world around it like the yeast in the measures of flour. In other words, the essential features of church life are worship, education, fellowship and outreach.

Of these activities, the most typical and the most central is that of worship. The derivation of this word and its association with values have already been discussed; here it may be sufficient to say that worship is essentially a celebration of the values which the individual and the worshipping community see as ultimate in life. The word celebration is the one traditionally used in this connection; for example, in the Catholic tradition the priest celebrates Mass. Corporate worship is an attempt to celebrate and reintegrate into the lives of the participants the values that they have come to see as ultimate, whatever symbols, personal or otherwise, may be used to portray such values.

Such worship can easily degenerate into idolatrous forms when the values upon which it sets its focus fall short of being truly ultimate. Whatever becomes of paramount importance to the life of an individual or group is to that extent an object of worship, but where that object is chosen principally on account of its presumed usefulness to the worshipper, then the worship is at root self-centred. Into this category could be placed such common objects of worship as wealth and material possessions, power and fame. The more worthy objects are worshipped for their own sake, irrespective of their apparent usefulness. One gives oneself in service to them, instead of expecting to make them serviceable to oneself.

How does the highest worship find expression in practice? It will make full use of all the arts through which the human spirit can soar, and will be rich with symbols that point to far more than they directly state. A service of worship has been aptly compared to such an occasion as a wedding anniversary. The husband and wife go out together to dinner to celebrate. The dinner is more than simply an eating of food, just as a Christmas or birthday gift is more than a piece of merchandise. It is a symbolic act which brings into focus their consciousness and appreciation of their common life together, compounded as it is of shared memories, sentiments, explorations, hopes and endeavours. The outward observance expresses, deepens and strengthens their common life together.

In just the same way a church service, whatever its specific form, expresses not simply the shared life of two persons but the shared life of the entire congregation, with the memories, sentiments and aspirations that bind it together in one common life from generation to generation. If the service does not do this, then it becomes a perfunctory formality, or else a titillation of some passing or entertaining curiosity on the part of those gathered together. In either case, it degenerates into a show.

The variety of outlook and experience to be found within any Unitarian congregation poses real problems for the creation of an act of worship in which all can join with full integrity. It can be achieved only through an openness on the part of all concerned to many forms of expression, with no assumption of the finality of any of them. Few of the participants on a given occasion might choose precisely the same form if it were solely a matter of expressing their own personal preferences, but more often than is commonly recognized, expression may be given during the common worship to something the individual may have wanted to express but did not quite know how.

The worship of a group of people who know, understand and respect each other always embodies values that are not there for the individual in isolation. Such values can be destroyed by the exaggerated individualism which, here as elsewhere, is the enemy of community. The freedom and integrity of the individual cannot be preserved through an attempt to make the group observance into something which is just as he or she personally would have designed it. This is an impossible demand, for it could be met only by overriding the wishes of someone else. The solution lies in the cultivation of a flexibility which can accept alternative forms of expression for what is, at root, the same underlying response to life. It involves also a recognition on the part of each individual that one's own personal way of expressing this religious response, though not necessarily included in the group observance, is always respected. The situation thus differs completely from that in a church where a stereotyped service inherited from the past can be imposed upon those present without regard for the way they actually feel.

Alfred North Whitehead laid his finger on the truth when he wrote, "That religion is strong which in its rituals and modes of thought evokes an apprehension of the commanding vision."[1] This vision will take different forms for different people, but where there is a genuine spirit of mutual acceptance, it is the group experience growing and flowing in combination with individual diversities that will determine its outward expression. It cannot be imposed. It can only grow. Where it does grow, no words or forms will be sacrosanct. It will be a matter of finding the most natural, realistic, beautiful and effective forms of expression into which all can enter as wholeheartedly as possible to "evoke an apprehension of the commanding vision."

The nature of the group will determine which forms of worship are most appropriate. One factor is age. The forms of worship most effective for small children will in general be considerably more informal, spontaneous and less influenced by historical continuity than the forms for adults. Where children are involved together with adults in one service, there has to be a greater emphasis upon movement, colour and dramatic forms to allow for the children's more limited span of concentration.

A second governing factor is that of size. The smaller the group, the more informal and spontaneous the observance, though even for the individual alone there are recognized forms and procedures that have been tested and passed down from the past. These can be of real help to

---

[1] A. N. Whitehead, *Science and the Modern World* (Cambridge, 1932), 239.

Dimensions of Community

worship at a personal level as long as (and only as long as) they make a definite connection with realities known and felt in personal experience. The larger the group becomes, the larger the dependence upon structure and form, and the more important it is that these be ordered in harmony and beauty. The same is true in any type of artistic appreciation: the larger the number of people involved, the greater the need for structure in the proceedings, so that they have a beauty of their own. It is not for nothing that the expression Order of Service is used; in a world which is radically disordered, a religious service is one occasion on which we can rediscover the beauties inherent in order and harmony. This is only another way of saying that there is an effort to live in the spirit of the whole, and that this whole is an ordered whole. Worship is the response to it with heart and soul and mind and strength, bringing the entire congregation together in one united act.

Education, as the second major function of the congregation, has obvious points of continuity with its worship. In both there is an exploration of reality. The emphasis in worship, however, lies upon celebration, aspiration and commitment. In education the dominant notes are inquiry, investigation, interpretation of experience and discussion of ideas. Organized religion has had a long association with education. In fact, there have been times and places where the only systems of formal education in existence were entirely under ecclesiastical auspices. Down to the present day the interest of religious bodies in public systems of education has continued, though it has often taken the form of pressure to secure the teaching of specific theological doctrines in the schools, either directly or by implication.

Unitarians have resisted such pressure to use public education as a vehicle for indoctrination. Not only does this inhibit the flowering of personal religion out of a direct response to experienced realities; it also encourages Thwackum definitions by presenting to the public mind a truncated picture of what religion is. Systems of "religious education" have usually taken the form of instruction in the history, mythology, rituals and ethics of specific forms of organized religion. The view has thus been popularized that religion is concerned with a particular class of subjects in which a person may or may not be interested, rather than an overall response to life in which every person is inextricably involved.

Moreover, the traditional approach to religious education fosters the view that there is one correct and assured set of answers to life's basic problems, in the acceptance of which a person can find complete and lasting security. But time has a way of eroding such dogmatic certainty, and a more realistic approach to religious education will accept uncertainty and insecurity as perennial features of the human condition. People have to be helped to live in a world of change; a world, moreover, in which many interpretations of reality and of our place in it will continue to coexist side by side. Religious education has to help equip those it touches to live in the world as it is, and the world as it is contains uncertainty, change, and rival systems of thought.

Each one of us has to accept personal responsibility for charting a course through such a world, notwithstanding the help one may find in such a setting as that of a Unitarian congregation. It would be foolish for any system of religious education to deliberately ignore the existence of organized traditions of public religion, but they make their presence felt so effectively that the greater danger is that religion will come to be thought of as an aspect of life limited to the channels they have marked out. Unitarian religious education, while by no means ignoring history, biography, mythology, and traditional ways of thinking, bases itself squarely upon a first-hand personal encounter with life, which is going to be different for each individual.

Religion for each one of us is our response to what we have thus far learned of life. Religious education will provide opportunities for further learning, and will help each person clarify and interpret his or her experience of life. It will provide a vehicle by means of which different interpretations can be compared and discussed, both the interpretations of those involved in the discussion and the interpretations which have been handed down from various sources in the past. Lastly, it will provide a setting in which the social dimensions of religion can be experienced and explored. There will therefore be no attempt at indoctrination, but rather a full and free examination of the questions posed by human experience of the adventure of living. This examination will include an attempt to ascertain the extent of our real knowledge about the nature of things. The whole of this exploration will be undertaken not only in a spirit of scientific inquiry, but also with that spirit of wonder which, according to Socrates, is the beginning of wisdom. It will search for an understanding of personal relationships between human beings. It will examine the varied interpretations of life that have been handed down through the world's great religions. All these form part of a meaningful system of religious education, and all gain in scope and value through being undertaken within the community life of the congregation.

This shared enterprise of the congregation also enables each individual to find the perspective within which to place the varied influences which make their effect felt. The inherited beliefs and example of family, neighbourhood or nation, the impact of the mass media of modern communication, beliefs and value-systems inculcated through organized systems of public education: all these have to be evaluated by any person who wants to build an authentic personal religion. Within the free atmosphere of the congregation this can take place, as traditional ideas are weighed, moral issues discussed and value-systems forged out of a genuine response to the facts of life-experience.

A congregation is not normally the only group in which values are formed in this way. The natural unit which usually enters into the community of congregational life is that of the family. The role of the church is to build upon and place within a broader setting the exploration into beliefs and values which is always going on in a family where fundamental questions about life are asked. If there is no such discussion in a family, it is not for lack of opportunity. The questions come up in a steady stream from all children who have not been inhibited from asking them. In trying to come to grips with questions the children raise, parents find that they and the children are learning together, and each from one another. It is not simply a matter of passing on accumulated wisdom from one generation to the next. In fact, it is surprising how often parents find they have not clarified their own thinking until they are pressed for answers by their children.

Within the congregation, as in the family, educational activities embrace all ages. No one is too young or too old, too learned or too cut off from others. None the less, the most appropriate ways of expressing this in practice will vary from one person to another, and most obviously the procedures suitable for adults will differ from those suitable for children.

There have been people who have taken issue with the whole procedure of involving children within the framework of congregational life in this way, because the children are being brought; they are not yet in the position of making a free decision of their own. Some people, in fact, claim that they will give their children no religious education. Let the children wait, they say, until they have reached an age when they can make rational choices of their own, and then let them choose their religion for themselves.

At first sight such an attitude seems very liberal and unbiased, but in fact it is completely unrealistic. It is just not possible for parents to give a child no religious education at all. They may refuse to let the child go anywhere near a place of worship. They may even try to control his or her access to reading material, television and the internet, but what they cannot avoid is the influence of the things said and done every day in the home, the values by which the adults in that home actually live, their giving or not giving of themselves to what is felt to be of worth (in other words, their worship). Actions speak louder than words. Attitudes do not have to be conveyed through conventional religious or moral teachings. They are picked up unconsciously, and all parents are teachers of religion whether they like it or not.

The same is true of influences outside the home. These, in their varying ways and degrees, all contribute to the child's religious education. Their contribution may reinforce that of the home or may run counter to it. But it is inescapable, and the only responsible way of handling the situation is to work consciously to help the child develop the knowledge, attitudes and values which go into the making of an authentic personal religion. This is a process in which a free and undogmatic congregation can be of enormous help.

The process begins at birth. Religious education is a lifelong enterprise. The first few years of a child's life illustrate more vividly than any others how inextricably religion is interwoven with the whole of life. At the outset, children lack all the apparatus of verbal communication, yet they are continually responding to the setting in which they find themselves, absorbing the atmosphere of love and security – or their absence. Their earliest years are generally spent almost exclusively at home, and here the influence of the home is at a maximum. The role of the congregation at this point is indirect: it helps the parents frame a meaningful religion of their own, which will include an understanding of the basic life-demands of the tiny child.

From the age of about three years the church can become involved more directly, though the main channel through which it communicates with the child is still the home. In an organized setting at the church, for a short time each week, a child can explore with others of the same age the mystery of unfolding life and knowledge, and build relationships with other people. Many of the people involved in the planning and running of this side of the children's educational program will be parents themselves. It is a cooperative enterprise, but one in which the congregation as a whole feels involved.

As children grow older and their horizons broaden, the formal educational program at the church explores not only their own shared wonderings and relationships, but also the whole of the human community's response to life, past and present, that has gone under the name of religion. From stories and myths, biography and dramatic reenactments, children explore ideas about life and its meaning and begin to articulate their own value-systems. But the home still stands in a paramount position in helping children form authentic and religiously defensible value-systems. Home and church have to continue in close cooperation, particularly in view of the shallow conventional value-systems bombarding children as well as adults in modern society.

If the genuine values of love, goodwill, tolerance, justice and peace are to become effective realities rather than catchwords and slogans, there have to be places where their meaning is explored in a free and practical way. The home and the church are such places, and they have to work together. It is not easy to be a nonconformist, and those who challenge the conventional values of society in the name of something higher stand in need of all the support they can get. Adults do, and even more, children do.

Unitarians have a centuries-long tradition of creative nonconformity. Within the congregation and within the homes associated with the congregation, the young person struggling to become an authentic individual in a world which sets no premium upon such authenticity can receive encouragement and support.

Home and church interact, therefore, at each age-level. Even for older children who can have a vigorous and productive community life of their own at the church, the religious influences of the home are important. The parents can help by developing and expressing their own values, and by participating in study and discussion at the church to reach a fuller understanding of the patterns of their children's religious growth. No clear line of division can be drawn between their involvement as parents and their involvement as adults in their own right; the two are intimately connected. In just the same way each demands reading, study, discussion, questioning, listening to presentations of ideas and concerns, and continuous practice in the art of living itself. Children's education and adult education are closely interwoven. The church is an intergenerational learning and teaching community.

A further dimension is added both to worship and to education by the fact that these take place within the fellowship of a congregation. They thus differ quite markedly from seemingly similar activities that take place in other contexts. Sir Adrian Boult, who was a leading Unitarian as well as one of the foremost musical conductors of the twentieth century, pointed out that in a period when conventional religious observances were declining, many younger people were finding an alternative source of spiritual uplift through attendance at concerts. Yet it remains true that although a concert audience may be deeply moved by the experiences shared during an evening together, it is still no more than an assembly of individuals with no ongoing life as a community. The same is true of an audience attending a lecture in adult education. Any relationships that exist between those who merely sit side by side are usually specialized and temporary.

By contrast, a congregation which is functioning as it should brings people together over a long period of time and at many levels of their lives. It is more than an organization; it is an organism. The traditional metaphor is the one used by Paul the Apostle: "Just as in a single human body there are many limbs and organs, all with different functions, so all of us form one body, serving individually as limbs and organs to one another. There are many members, but one body … If one member suffers, they all suffer together. If one flourishes, they all rejoice together."[2]

---

[2] Romans 12: 4-5; 1 Corinthians 12: 20, 26.

Dimensions of Community

Each member within the body has its own identity, its own integrity, its own function to perform, its own contribution to make. Together they sustain the whole. In fact, they constitute the whole, for without the members the body has no existence of its own. Yet the functioning of the body as a whole has a quality which is something other than the sum of the functioning of all the individual members. This synergy has a strength and vitality that is all its own.

The third of the four quadrants into which the life of a congregation can be divided finds its focus here. In recent years there has been considerable emphasis upon the church as a caring and sharing community, which can combat the feelings of rootlessness experienced by so many people in the contemporary world, and can do so without demanding an acceptance of creeds and dogmas that are inconsistent with intellectual integrity. But there is still need for caution. It is easy to become sentimental in one's expectations and to forget that, however warm and nurturing a religious community may appear to be, it is still composed of people who are very human.

The German philosopher Arthur Schopenhauer once told a parable. On a cold winter's day, so cold that one could freeze to death, a group of animals tried to huddle together to keep warm. The problem was that these animals were porcupines. As soon as they got too close to each other they found that this was just as uncomfortable as being too cold. So they moved in and out again repeatedly until they discovered the best distance at which they could keep each other warm without puncturing each other's skins.

The porcupines offer a better parable of human community than furry, cuddly little animals would do. None the less, Schopenhauer's story is inadequate. The reason why the porcupines huddled together was simply to escape from the cold. While warmth is a valuable outcome of religious community, it is not the chief end in view. Community that is sought only because it can engender warmth for people who would otherwise feel shut out in the cold may seem to work or a while, but ultimately it always fails. It has to gather around a centre that has meaning and gives meaning to the lives of its members, and it has also to face actively outward into the life of the larger world.

The idea of a cloistered religion shut away from the world outside has always been foreign to Unitarian thinking. There have been times and places when Unitarians have attempted to live communally, sharing much of their lives and possessions with each other – Raków in sixteenth-century Poland, for example, or Brook Farm in nineteenth-century Massachusetts – but these communities kept up an intimate and active involvement in the world at large. Unitarians would endorse the sentiments expressed by Saint-Exupéry: "Life has taught us that love does not consist in gazing at each other, but in looking outward together in the same direction. There is no comradeship except through union in the same high effort."[3]

When the porcupines face in the same direction, their quills can be laid back in parallel lines rather than wrecking the attempt to live in community. Joys and sorrows, hopes and disillusionments, work and commitment can be shared as parts of a many-sided community life that expresses religion as inter-personal relationship. When this happens, relationships with the surrounding world are enhanced rather than inhibited.

These wider relationships are the focal concern in the fourth quadrant of congregational life. Here the community seeks ways to respond to its call to social responsibility. This flows directly out of the worship in which its dedication to ultimate values is celebrated and reinforced, and also from its educational process, for only well-informed and thoughtful involvement will make a positive contribution to the life of the world. Without such a background of reflection and discussion, action can often be counterproductive. It may be no more than a pursuit of self-interest or shallow enthusiasms under the cloak of noble-sounding verbiage. It may be simply a knee-jerk reaction against what others say or do, in which case (as when the same thing happens in theological argument) it is parasitical upon that which it opposes. Or again, it may simply mean jumping aboard someone else's bandwagon because the announced destination sounds like the right one, without pausing to ask whether the proposed route for reaching that destination is really acceptable in the light of the religious principles to which one is committed. An authentic expression of religion at an active level in human society demands that one be well equipped both with a firm

---

[3] Antoine de Saint-Exupéry, *Wind, Sand and Stars* (New York, 1945), 231.

grasp of such principles and with an accurate assessment of the situation to which they are to be applied.

Social responsibility can find expression in two practical forms. As is usually true of such distinctions, the line of division between the two is not absolutely clear-cut, but in general it is possible to distinguish between social service on the one hand and social action on the other. Social service accepts the existing social structure and sets out within that structure to help people who for one reason or another stand in need of help. Social action, on the other hand, sets out to help others by changing the social structure, or by advocating such change. It may involve speaking out against evils that are institutionalized in the framework of society, and in supporting those who work for reform.

For example, unemployment has long been recognized as a social evil. In face of widespread unemployment, social service might take the form of organizing soup kitchens and food banks, making church leadership and premises available for creative projects to combat the demoralizing effect of long-term enforced idleness, or trying to assist individuals in finding employment. Such efforts could all be useful and productive. Social action, on the other hand, would be more likely to take the form of bearing witness publicly to the perversion of values in a society which accepts mass unemployment, and of working through whatever channels are available to promote the structural changes in society that are calculated to give human values priority over economic values.

There will always be a need for social service. However good or bad a social order may be, there will always be persons within it in circumstances of special need. Sometimes they may best be helped on a person-to-person basis, sometimes it is better to set up an organization as a more effective tool. Large numbers of voluntary societies exist for this purpose, and churches have usually regarded such work as a natural expression of their religious commitment.

Unitarians have had a distinguished record in this field, so much so that the story of what was done in the past presents a perpetual challenge to Unitarians in the present. But seldom have they rested content with social service alone. Social action has been an equally prominent undertaking, and this has inevitably carried both individuals and congregations into far more controversial areas. Criticism of the existing social, economic or political order is always bound to arouse resentment from those who are, on the whole, satisfied with things as they are.

Movements for social reform during the past few centuries have almost always had Unitarians working prominently in them, often spearheading the movement. The list of issues tackled is a long and quite spectacular one, including the abolition of slavery and of discriminatory practices against ethnic and religious minorities; the establishment of civil liberties; reform of unrepresentative governments at all levels; extension of the franchise; provisions for equality of status between the sexes; the establishment of comprehensive systems of public education; improvement of working conditions in industry and social insurance; reform of the treatment of criminals and of those suffering from physical or mental illness; promotion of peace and international understanding – these are some of the more outstanding examples.

Such issues provided themes for innumerable sermons and discussions in the churches, but the practical activities were usually undertaken by individual members of those churches. They did not necessarily announce themselves as such, but the enemies of reform had no difficulty in identifying where the seeds were sown. More than one Unitarian place of worship in eighteenth-century England was sacked by the mob and burned to the ground, often with the tacit approval of the civil authorities. Similar attacks have taken place in the United States.

Extreme reactions of this kind, however deplorable, are certainly understandable. There is a widespread feeling, particularly among those who stand to benefit from a continuation of the status quo, that "the church shouldn't meddle in politics" – or economics, or social life generally. Religion, it is claimed, is strictly an individual concern, and the life of the individual can be divorced from the life of society. Evangelical piety sets its focus upon a transformation of the individual, arguing that if the lives of enough individuals are changed, the life of society will change too. Evolutionary theory, on the other hand, suggests that an organism adapts to its habitat. Provide a fiercely competitive environment and you develop aggressive characteristics within the individual. Provide a cooperative environment, and you will foster the development of love and mutual aid. This point of view has long historical antecedents. It was the basis of what was proclaimed by the Hebrew prophets of old.

Dimensions of Community

Where do Unitarians stand in this debate? Few would see the alternatives as mutually exclusive, and even fewer would see the church as having no role in promoting social progress. But what should that role be? There is no question but that it should include developing an awareness among church members both of basic religious principles and of the social context to which they should be applied. Nor would there be much controversy over the proposition that the church should apply them. The real issue arises when one asks just what "the church" really means in such a context. In one sense, to speak of the church is simply a convenient way of referring collectively to all the individuals who compose it, and who are just as truly "the church" when involved in their own daily activities as when they gather in community. In this sense, if individual Unitarians take action on social concerns, then the church is taking action.

But is this enough? A community is more than an aggregation of individuals. It has a corporate life and identity of its own, which embodies the contribution not only of present members, but of those who have gone before them. How far can that corporate identity be directly involved in projects in social responsibility? Does the congregation as such take a public stand?

In the past, this was seldom done, for several reasons. The first was the desire of concerned Unitarians to work closely with all who shared their concern, no matter what their religious motivation. To fly a denominational flag as they went into action might provoke unnecessary divisions by raising irrelevant issues, so where they worked as part of a group they preferred it to be one in which people of every persuasion could work together for a common goal. This argument is still a powerful one. From the point of view of getting things done, organizations which can bring everyone sharing a concern together are to be preferred to separate organizations set up on the basis of religious or other divisions. What a church can do is to pioneer the way in fields where there are no existing organizations, handing over the work to a community-wide organization as soon as possible. Furthermore, where a matter of public concern calls for as many voices as possible to be heard, the voice of individuals can be supplemented by that of the church as a whole, which in some circles at any rate will command respect on account of the principles the church is assumed to represent.

But if the church is to speak, it must be able to do so with one voice. This means that there has to be a general consensus within the congregation on the point at issue. The second reason why individual action was preferred in the past was that social action by the church as a whole is liable to collide with the principle of individual freedom and responsibility, upon which Unitarians have laid such stress. Action in the name of the group has somehow to be reconciled with the basis of that group as a creedless congregation – and "creedless" covers social and political creeds as well as theological ones. None of the members must be made to feel that their freedom of belief and action is being violated, and even where there is a consensus in the congregation there is seldom complete unanimity. How is corporate action to be undertaken consistently with the rights of a dissenting minority?

In the past, action in the name of the congregation as a whole was frequently checked or halted as it came up against this obstacle. This happened in all aspects of the congregational life: worship, education and fellowship as well as outreach. Dissent by individuals or small but vocal minorities has had the effect of altering or inhibiting policies and practices acceptable to the majority. But the issues encountered in the field of social action often tend to arouse stronger feelings than those encountered elsewhere.

Basically, the question is once again that of the responsible exercise of individuality in such a way that it does not damage the community. It should be understood and made clear that declarations or actions reflecting a consensus in the congregation do not in any sense limit the right of an individual to dissent. Such a right is fundamental in a fellowship based upon the principle of unity in diversity. Furthermore, the dissenter should be freely able to make the attempt to change the consensus by rational argument. Often enough in the past the minority point of view in one generation has become the majority point of view in the next. But given these safeguards and opportunities, the dissenter should not try to thwart the open expression of an existing broad consensus within the congregation on matters of current concern.

On the other hand, the majority, however overwhelming, has responsibilities as well. It has to assess the number of dissenters and the importance to the issue to them. It has to balance against this the importance of the issue to the congregation as a whole and to society at large. Finally it has to weigh both its own position and that of the dissenters in the light of the basic principles of the church. Where a position is obviously in conflict with the church's avowed principles it rejects itself automatically. For instance, the principle of a free, open and inclusive community automatically invalidates points of view that are unfree, closed and exclusive, such as chauvinism based upon race, sex or nationality. Totalitarianism, whether of the right or of the left, is unacceptable. This is not to argue that totalitarianism is all of a kind. Totalitarianism of the left is less ultimately destructive than totalitarianism of the right, because its motivations and objectives are good, though its methodology is bad. In totalitarianism of the right, both the motivations and the methodology are bad.

An exclusive, rigid, totalitarian person cannot claim minority rights in an open, free, inclusive congregation. The principle of inclusiveness automatically excludes such a person's exclusiveness. But most situations of dissent within a congregation are far less clear-cut than this. They more often involve an apparent conflict of principles all of which command general support, rather than the straightforward application of one principle. Unitarians, for instance, generally affirm the principles of personal freedom, of reverence for life, of protection of the innocent against arbitrary violence. The reconciliation of these and other principles has in recent years resulted in a general consensus against capital punishment and in favour of making the question of abortion a matter of personal conscience for the woman concerned, with whatever consultation may be indicated. In neither case is there unanimity. And, it should be added, in neither case do most people come effortlessly to a firm decision.

To put it personally, for many years I have taken a stand in opposition to capital punishment. Yet there have been situations where I have had to confront a welter of uncertainty as to whether it would not really be better for everyone concerned, including the offender, if that person were permanently removed from society. In other words, there is a minority report within myself too, and I have to recognize that it is there. But it would be a dereliction of my social responsibility to use this as an excuse for taking no action when an issue confronts me. I have to respond to the moral demand to take a stand on capital punishment or on abortion, but that stand expresses the outcome of an inner wrestling with all the tragedy inherent in the situation. After such a wrestling, it is hard to deal unsympathetically with someone who has gone through the same process and has come out on the opposite side of the issue.

All these factors have to be taken into consideration when a congregation takes a stand on a social issue. Yet it remains possible for such a stand to be taken without violating the integrity of dissenters, just as it remains possible for corporate worship to take place without violating the integrity of theological dissenters. Various procedures are open. First of all, there must always be a full and fair hearing of all points of view before a stand is taken. More often than many people realize, it is possible for that stand to take account of the initial concerns expressed by objectors without detracting from the essential thrust of the action.

Secondly, if there is a vote, the result of that vote should be public information, just as is the result of a vote in a legislature or parliament. If a congregation sends a brief to some level of government that was passed by majority vote at a meeting, an indication of that vote would probably mean that the submission would be considered more seriously by the recipient. It would show that at least that many people took the time and trouble to grapple seriously with the issue. If the figures were embarrassing, either because the vote was close or because the total was very small, then the communication should probably not be sent in the name of the congregation at all. And the fact that the minority vote is recorded means that it is not deprived of a voice.

It may be that there is only a narrow path, to be trodden with care, between a cowardly silence and a foolish babbling. But for the voice of calm reason there will always sooner or later be a hearing. And if a Unitarian congregation can gain the reputation of speaking with such a voice, it will continue to exercise, as Unitarian congregations have so often done in the past, an influence disproportionate to the size of its membership.

Outreach therefore ranks along with worship, education and fellowship as an indispensable function of the congregation as such. Wherever these four aspects of congregational life are all effectively present and interacting, there the congregation is alive and provides a balanced community life for its members. To this a Unitarian congregation adds a broad inclusiveness, a questioning and undogmatic spirit and an attempt to take constant account of developing knowledge. Such a combination will be found in few other places, and vindicates the existence of a Unitarian religious organization.

www.ingramcontent.com/pod-product-compliance
Lightning Source LLC
Chambersburg PA
CBHW050554300426
44112CB00013B/1913